MICHAEL CHIAGO

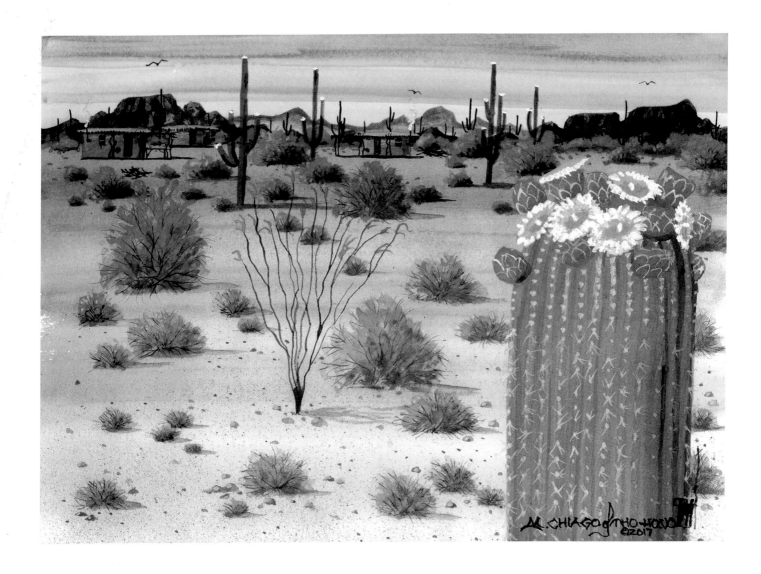

The Southwest Center Series
Jeffrey M. Banister, Editor

MICHAEL CHIAGO

O'odham Lifeways Through Art

PAINTINGS BY MICHAEL CHIAGO SR.
TEXT BY AMADEO M. REA

THE UNIVERSITY OF
ARIZONA PRESS

TUCSON

The University of Arizona Press
www.uapress.arizona.edu

We respectfully acknowledge the University of Arizona is on the land and territories of Indigenous peoples. Today, Arizona is home to twenty-two federally recognized tribes, with Tucson being home to the O'odham and the Yaqui. Committed to diversity and inclusion, the University strives to build sustainable relationships with sovereign Native Nations and Indigenous communities through education offerings, partnerships, and community service.

ISBN-13: 978-0-8165-4475-2 (paperback)

Cover design by Leigh McDonald
Cover art by Michael Chiago Sr.
Designed and typeset by Leigh McDonald in Berkeley Oldstyle 11/15, Tallow Sans TC and Good Headline Pro (display)

Publication of this book is made possible in part by financial support from the Southwest Center of the University of Arizona, and by the proceeds of a permanent endowment created with the assistance of a Challenge Grant from the National Endowment for the Humanities, a federal agency.

Library of Congress Cataloging-in-Publication Data
Names: Chiago, Michael, artist. | Rea, Amadeo M., author.
Title: Michael Chiago : O'odham lifeways through art / paintings by Michael Chiago Sr. ; text by Amadeo M. Rea.
Description: Tucson : University of Arizona Press, 2022. | Series: Southwest Center series | Includes bibliographical references and index.
Identifiers: LCCN 2021053093 | ISBN 9780816544752 (paperback)
Subjects: LCSH: Chiago, Michael, Sr.—Appreciation. | Tohono O'odham Indians—Sonoran Desert—Social life and customs—Pictorial works.
Classification: LCC E99.P25 C45 2022 | DDC 979.1004/974552—dc23/eng/20211202
LC record available at https://lccn.loc.gov/2021053093

Printed in the United States of America
♾ This paper meets the requirements of ANSI/NISO Z39.48-1992 (Permanence of Paper).

CONTENTS

FOREWORD

WHEN I ARRIVED IN THE Sonoran Desert of southern Arizona to study the natural world and lizard biology as a young graduate student, I needed guidance. I looked for my place in it. The Native people who came long before me had wisdom—deep, with respect. Indigenous artists like Michael Chiago Sr. have maintained and expanded those connections, capturing revelations that have been nourished and simmered through generations of craft, insight, genius, cultural spirituality, and social commitment. Early on, I bought a painting by Michael. Some feeling told me it captured his people's essence of living here—his art has long fulfilled this role.

Years later, I visited my friend Dr. Amadeo Rea, ornithologist and ethnobiologist, and our conversation led to my love of Chiago's paintings. I discovered Michael had been one of Amadeo's high school students. He knew his paintings and his cultural world well, having written four books about O'odham and long-recalled stories of the birds, mammals, and plants inhabiting their desert and riverine landscapes. A unique collaboration offered itself: some of Chiago's visual depictions of his people's rich culture, if joined with Amadeo's insightful commentaries, could capture his people's way of life in the profound richness of our desert home.

Michael Chiago Sr. grew up surrounded by landscapes, the xeric plants and animals of the Sonoran Desert. He grew up immersed in a culture that had matured here from times beyond the cultural memory of family or friends. He has lived ingesting this atmosphere, visualizing its moods with cultural individuality. He details life among his people as they hold to their lifeways of wisdom, ceremony, and respect for the encircling environment—this land from which the O'odham have of course emerged and depended on for daily food and water for millennia in some of the driest broad stretches of North America.

Chiago captures some of the attributes his ancestors and fellow descendants have beautifully created, kept alive, and passed down. Each year the calendar they follow is followed by all life on Earth, as Earth circles the single Sun that provides the light that sustains life for us all. The people watch the plants that nourish and heal them, and with which they share the desert and their crucial need for rains. The Saguaro cactus bloom then fruit, Cholla buds sprout on spiny, swollen branches—both signal the hoped-for annual arrival of more abundant foods. These events indicate the approach of monsoon rains and upcoming family plantings of corn, squash, and tepary beans. Scattered people gather to join in ceremony, ensuring good fortune will come.

Michael Chiago Sr.'s paintings celebrate blessings the People solemnize while they support each other. From the use of song to garner spiritual forces to heal the sick to the dangerous trek south to bring home salt from the shores of vast, unending waters, all the necessities of life are depicted in Chiago's work. One painting shows tribe members, driven by hunger, surrounding, and grasping rabbits, while another shows people planting seeds in desert niches where rain waters may join the sun's rays to nurture food to share.

Beginning in the distant times of our species' origin, our lives have been enhanced by food and recounted tales around the hearth. Similarly, Michael Chiago Sr.'s visual portrayals bring glimpses to us all of his people living with intimacy within—and as part of—the Sonoran Desert.

—*Wade C. Sherbrooke*
September 7, 2021

PREFACE

THE MIDWIFE OF THIS WORK is Wade C. Sherbrooke. I was staying at his house one day while working in Tucson when he quite out of the blue said that someone needs to write a book about Michael Chiago Sr., the O'odham artist. It's an idea Wade had been toying with for about ten years, but every proposal so far had fallen through for some reason. You're the person most qualified to do it, he told me. I already had written four books on the Pima and Papago or the Akimel O'odham and Tohono O'odham, as they are known in their own language, and was working on a couple new books on the same. I didn't need more projects.

I thought about it for a few minutes and told Wade I had an idea about how this might be done. Michael as an artist was visually interpreting his culture through the medium of his paintings, just as an ethnographer interprets a culture through the lens of the written word. If I were to write a book on him, I would want to study his paintings and describe what is coming through his eyes.

Michael was in his senior year when I first came to the Franciscan-run St. John's Indian School in Komaḍk (Komatke), Arizona, in 1963. He graduated in the spring of 1964. I didn't teach seniors that year, but I counted some good friends in that class.

Wade was promptly looking up Michael's phone number out on the reservation. "Wait! Let me think about this." Too late. He had Michael on the line. "I've got someone here who wants to talk to you." He handed me the phone. "Mike, this is Amadeo Rea. I used to be Frater Amadeo at St. John's. You probably don't remember me."

"Of course I remember you! I was your barber in my senior year, and you always wanted a flat top and you wanted it short."

It had been more than fifty years since I had last talked to Michael. But we were soon down to the nuts and bolts of how I envisioned the project unfolding: We would assemble paintings that he did of O'odham life, I would write up what I saw in them, and then we'd sit down and go over both the painting and the text together, adding whatever I had overlooked. If there was an important aspect of his culture that he had not yet painted, he would do so. He thought this a workable process.

The philosophical basis for this process in anthropology is quite simple: The person who lives within the culture can explain and interpret it from the inside. The underlying value system is often understood by the insider. This is called the emic perspective. The ethnographer can observe the culture from the outside and ask questions. This is called the etic perspective.[1] Michael paints from the inside looking out; I write from the outside looking in. What the outsider observes may not be the same as what the insider is aware of, and the reverse is also true. Working together can provide congruence between the two perspectives. We hope that is the case for the images and verbal depictions in this book.

What emerges from this selection of Michael Chiago Sr.'s paintings is a virtually comprehensive picture of O'odham culture, focused primarily on the Tohono O'odham, who live in environments away from permanent desert rivers. First we get a view of the environmental setting of the People; then we see some of the major subsistence activities—wild harvesting, hunting, agriculture—that supplied the O'odham with their daily fare. The next set of paintings lets us into the everyday lives of the People going about their daily activities; one painting depicts life in a precontact environment.

Village saints' days are important annual highlights among both Tohono and Akimel O'odham. Through centuries of contact, the O'odham have evolved their own sets of religious and social activities around their feast days. Four of Michael's paintings depict such scenes.

The O'odham inhabit a landscape charged with the numinous: mountains, springs, oceans, ancient shrines honoring some special burial. Three images touch on this subject. When visiting these places, O'odham are expected to leave some votive offering: cornmeal, a bead, a coin, a polished stone, a sprig of Creosote Bush, even some drinking water splashed from a plastic bottle.

The O'odham have a belief that power can be obtained from a spiritual helper or "meeter." An encounter with a meeter can provide an individual with success in a way of life or with sung poetry. Songs are also power. Two of the paintings show the ocean, another source of power, and two more show aspects of shamanism and healing. But power can be turned to evil: one painting shows a ceremony of cleansing after a bad shaman has sent evil to the village.

---

1. These terms are derived from phon*etics*, the study of the total range of sounds that humans make, and phon*emics*, the culturally selected range of sounds that a language actually uses.

Rain is what makes plant and animal life possible in the desert. The People were not passive recipients of this life-giving water; various O'odham ceremonies with their incorporated dances are intended ultimately to bring rain. Michael illustrates four of these.

Cultures are entities with porous boundaries. Participants select and reject from surrounding cultures. The dominant outside influences on the O'odham have been Hispanic and Anglo-American; the impacts of this cultural exchange are taken up in eight paintings. They deal with diet, health, housing, education, economy, and government, in addition to the religious syncretism seen in the previous set of paintings depicting saints' days.

For centuries—but most notably during the European Renaissance—artists have interpreted biblical scenes in the contexts of their own cultures. Michael was asked to paint a set of the fourteen Stations of the Cross for a local church. He put the scenes of the Via Dolorosa in the context of O'odham culture much as Botticelli, the Brueghels, or Caravaggio did for their own cultures in their own times. One of the stations, the fourteenth, is reproduced here.

As I began writing, it soon became apparent that in addition to the visual and verbal ethnographic descriptions of Michael's culture for the general reader, there was something else of importance here. As with most Indigenous cultures around the world, the Tohono and Akimel O'odham are suffering from cultural and lin-guistic erosion. Michael paints the recent past of his parents' and grandparents' generations. Many of the scenes depict activities still found in everyday life on the reservations; other activities are no longer part of daily life. The language that goes with the activities both past and current is rapidly being lost among younger gen-erations. Here was an opportunity to make various linguistic aspects of the culture available for teaching in O'odham schools.

This presented a problem. There is dialectical variation among the O'odham. I work mostly with the Akimel O'odham, and the Koahadk and some other northern villages in the area speak an Akimel O'odham dialect. However, Michael speaks one of the dialects of Tohono O'odham. So we have tried to include in the text variants of both major dialects so the work is useful to a broader spectrum of O'odham students. One of the major variants is with the bilabial fricative consonant. Most Tohono O'odham will use /w/, whereas Akimel O'odham use /v/ for most words (*vaig*, 'three') and /w/ for others (*wuso*, 'to blow'; *wailla*, 'social dance'; *wupadaj*, 'cattail's flower stalk'; *wuagida*, 'girl's puberty ceremony').

Also, O'odham who write their language usually use a unigraphic orthography (one sound, one symbol). In two cases we have chosen to write out the sounds as digraphs: /sh/ and /ch/. This practical orthography will help avoid mispronuncia-tions among non-O'odham speakers.

O'odham words with an initial vowel begin with a glottal stop (*'O'odham* for instance). Since this is obligatory, it is understood; hence it has not been written here. Both Akimel and Tohono O'odham words are stressed on the first syllable of the base word, so again, the accent is understood and not written. (The accent is supplied on certain loan words that do not follow the rule.) Vowel length—that is, duration—is important in O'odham. Here long vowels are written double (*uus*, 'bush, stick'), while other orthographies write this as *u:s*.

Two sounds might give the English speaker problems. The /ɛ/ is a /u/ sound with the lips spread instead of rounded. The sound with the rounded lips is written /u/. The /l/ in O'odham words sounds much like /r/ (the apical alveolar lateral flap), similar to the /r/ in Spanish.

Throughout the centuries of contact with Hispanic and Anglo cultures, O'odham place-names have been mispronounced, misaccented, and misspelled by these foreign cultures. We have tried to give them their correct O'odham renderings here. Some names will differ from those that appear on road signs and maps.

A few other terms require clarification: *Piman* is an adjective that refers to Akimel O'odham; Koahadk and Huhu'ula, their neighbors immediately the south; the Tohono O'odham (formerly Papago); the Hia ch-eḍ O'odham or Sand People; the true Pima Bajo of the Sonora lowlands, probably including the Chuuvĭ Koa'adam or Jackrabbit Eaters of Sonora. All these together were known as the Northern Pimans, a formerly contiguous group; they are now more commonly known as O'odham. Also included in the Piman domain are the Mountain Pima of the Sonoran and Chihuahuan uplands, although Mountain Pima is a separate language from that of the lowland Pimans; they call themselves O'ob rather than O'odham. Two other groups of Pimans have been labeled as Tepehuán by colonizers: the Northern Tepehuán of Chihuahua and the Southern Tepehuán (including the Tepecano) of Durango and adjacent states just to the south. Anthropologists and linguists have coined the word *Tepiman* to include all groups of Piman speakers. There are four separate languages in this complex—lowland Piman, Mountain Pima, Northern Tepehuán, and Southern Tepehuán—and there are dialectical subgroups among each of these four. Aboriginally more than nine-tenths of Tepiman country lay south of Arizona and the international border.

This is not an art book. Except for some cursory exploration of how Michael Chicago Sr. became an artist, there is no attempt to analyze him as an artist. He would be the first to acknowledge that he does not belong to any "school" of Native American art. Nor is there any attempt to analyze the aesthetics of his work. Instead, this is an exploration of how Michael sees and interprets his culture through painting rather than through writing. The final product here is a joint effort in seeing: one of us a painter, the other an ethnographer.

ACKNOWLEDGMENTS

WE ARE INDEBTED FIRST OF all to Wade C. Sherbrooke for initiating this project and keeping it on track when progress (all too frequently) seemed stymied.

Neither the artist nor the author nor the book's godfather have expertise in the realm of electronics. Luckily university students Taylor Burnell and Matolius Chase came to the rescue. They were responsible for scanning many of the illustrations and assembling these with the text.

When a new computer program threatened to take things into its own hands—an all too often occurrence—Linda Kleiner would bail Amadeo out of the impasses. The air of his office is blue.

Michael's daughter, Michelle Chiago, was the source of most digitized figures, particularly the large collection of paintings housed at Casa Grande. We especially want to thank Thomas Cole, a Casa Grande attorney, who originally commissioned Michael to do a large number of paintings; many from his personal collection are reproduced here (pages 19, 20, 21, 23, 24, 25 [both paintings], 39, 41, 55, 69, 70, 81, 90, and 100).

James Bialac, longtime supporter of Chiago's work and the work of other southwestern Native American artists, contributed to the publication of this work.

Dr. Harry J. Winters Jr. and Luis Barragán checked the spelling of O'odham terms. Culver Cassa also consulted on O'odham terms as well as other cultural matters. Native speaker Cassa was the final arbiter on linguistic matters.

ARTIST'S STATEMENT

S KEG TASH [GOOD DAY].

My name is Michael Chiago Sr. I'm a Native artist from Tohono O'odham Nation (aka "the Desert People"). I was born in Koahadk, a small village in southern Arizona. I'm the youngest of my parents' children. My father, Phillip Chiago, is from Lehi, Salt River Pima–Maricopa Indian Community (Arizona), and my mother, Amy Domingo-Chiago, is from the village of Ge Komalik on Tohono O'odham Nation (southern Arizona).

I spent a lot of time on the Tohono O'odham reservation with my grandmother and mother when I was a child growing up. There, they told me stories of our tribe. My mother would tell me the meanings of the old ceremonies they had seen and participated in themselves. That's also where, as a youth, I witnessed the daily life and ceremonies of our people.

Around the time I was born and grew up in, people lived simply, like in the 1930s and 1940s on the reservation. There was no running water; we hauled water in fifty-gallon drums from the village windmill. We used kerosene lamps and candles for lighting at night, and people were using horse-drawn wagons. These are all things I eventually used as inspiration for my artwork.

At a very young age I needed to leave home to live at a government-run boarding school for Native Americans. It was during this time I began drawing pictures. My pictures were of my home: desert scenes with mountains, cactus, and the sky with clouds. It wasn't until the second grade that I began getting recognition from classmates and teachers about my drawings. My class would have a drawing contest every Friday; I would always win. I will always remember the encouragement from my teacher telling me how good my drawings were and that I should go to art school.

I continued art on my own all throughout high school. That's when I started to do art with oil paint, but I never really liked it because it took so long to dry. That's when I moved on and started using watercolor paints because they were easy to blend and dried quickly.

After high school, I began to sell my artwork. I would paint different Native subject matter like kachinas and fancy dancers. Fancy dancing wasn't part of my culture, though I was familiar with it because I was involved in a traveling fancy dancing group at my high school that I got to travel with all around the United States. Then one day a customer asked me "Why don't you paint your tribe?" I sat there a moment and thought to myself, "Why not?" It had never occurred to me. It made me think of all the stories my mother told me about: ceremonies and life on the reservation I had experienced when I was a young boy. It was easy for me to visualize because it was my environment: the desert, the villages, the people.

The more I painted, the more the memories of everyday life, dances, and ceremonies flowed. These are the images I remember growing up with. It all influenced how I paint today.

Still, even years later I strive to be very detailed. I want it to look more realistic, how are clothes worn, how a cactus forms, or colors of the day. I like adding a lot of detail to my paintings.

It is now over fifty years I've been doing my artwork. I have lost track of the number of paintings I have completed; time has gone by fast. I'm still very busy with Indian art markets, classes I teach, demonstrations and such.

To all my family and all the people, customers, clients, and my fellow artists I've met during different markets and places I traveled around the world, I'd like to thank you for your support and for being there for me over the years.

I enjoyed every bit of it. I will continue to do artwork till the end.

—*Michael Chiago Sr.,*
Tohono O'odham artist

MICHAEL CHIAGO

INTRODUCTION

THE GENESIS OF AN ARTIST

W E ARE ALL BORN, I think, as naturalists and artists. As very small children, we have an intense interest in the natural world around us. And we have a drive to create. Give a child a crayon or pencil or paintbrush and a piece of paper, and their attention is riveted on the project. And the results are often admirable by any aesthetic standards. A caterpillar eating a flower elicits a similar intensity of attention.

But then comes school. Inexorably our attention is focused on more culturally accepted goals. Our primal interest in all the living things around us is downplayed by teachers concerned with instilling in their charges the "basics"—what were once called the three Rs. Our opportunities for hunting, growing crops, and gathering wild resources are limited to weekends, if even that. Often they are further restricted by urban living. Teachers' attitudes may not match our nascent interests. Our exuberant artistic drives get channeled into tamer lines and usually eliminated altogether. But sometimes, for those rare individuals, this never happens. Their childhood impulses thrive and are funneled into a career. These lucky individuals become artists and biologists of various sorts.

In 1943 a wagon left Lehi, the Maricopa village on the Salt River Pima–Maricopa Indian Community in Arizona (page 23). It carried a pregnant woman of Tohono O'odham descent and her husband, of mixed Onk Akimel O'odham and Piipaash (Maricopa) descent, as well as a number of other family members. The trip took several days (though it would be scarcely an hour or two with today's travel). The destination was the Koahadk village on the northern part of the Tohono O'odham Nation. The village had a good midwife. There Michael was born.

Michael was the fourth child. Already there was a sister ten years older, another older brother, and a brother just three years older than Michael. Scrounging a living was difficult. Before he started school, his parents worked in the cotton fields around Stanfield and later Casa Grande, Arizona (page 99). There were O'odham camps here, settled by various lineages and dialect groups. Because they moved around so much, Michael spent several years trying to get through the first grade. Eventually his parents sent him to the Santa Rosa Boarding School, where he was two years behind his age-mates.

Michael attributes his artistic awakening to his time in grades 1 through 7 at Santa Rosa Boarding School on the Tohono O'odham reservation. His second-grade teacher, Mrs. Audi May Morgan, recognized his budding talent and kept him supplied with art materials, mostly crayons but no paint. Every Thursday or Friday there was an art contest, and the students usually selected Michael's drawings as the best.

At the end of seventh grade, Michael transferred to St. John's Indian School in Komaḍk (Komatke), south of Phoenix. He continued here through his high school graduation in 1963–1964. He says that there were more outlets here for his artistic inclinations. Sister Bardell encouraged the eighth-grader's work. Some student work was sold in the Indian store in front of the church. In high school there was the Indians arts and crafts club, sponsored by Sister Antonine and Miss Mary Hanratty, and in his senior year he was able to visit the Scottsdale National Arts Exhibition with Thomas W. Fennell and me, where he was exposed to the work of other budding Native American artists of the 1960s, such as R. C. Gorman and Fritz Scholder.

Michael was in the drum and bugle corps in his freshman and sophomore years and was an avid basketball player, but age limitations (he was over eighteen) prevented him from playing varsity his last two years of high school. During his junior and senior years, Michael was an Indian dancer; he made his own dance costume, including cuffs and other beadwork pieces. His artwork in this period focused on fancy dancers. After graduation, he had an opportunity to travel to Massachusetts and to the 1964 New York World's Fair with his fellow Indian dancers.

An aside is necessary here for those not familiar with southwestern Indians: Native Americans have been grouped into broad geographic culture areas based on early studies by the father of American anthropology, Franz Boas. What comes to the minds of most non-Indians thinking about Native peoples is the Plains Indian culture area: feathered headdresses, clothing beaded with geometric designs, tipis, bison hunting, Plains music, powwows, and a Plains style of dancing. But there are other culture areas with equally distinct aesthetic standards and lifestyles such as the Pacific Northwest peoples or the Eastern Woodlands peoples.

The Native peoples of the Southwest have resisted any handy categorization. The O'odham, for instance, are not culturally like any of the Pueblo, Apache, or Navajo neighbors to the north. The affinities of the O'odham (and all Tepimans) are to the south: their cultural relatives are the Ópata, Yaqui, Mayo, Mountain

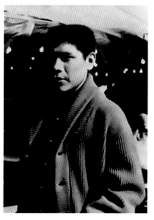

Michael Chiago Sr. as a high school senior, St. John's Indian School, 1963–1964. Photo by Thomas W. Fennell.

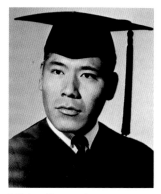

Michael's senior portrait. Photographer unknown.

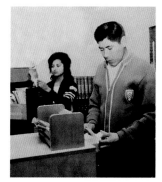

Michael with Agatha Manuel at St. John's Indian School, 1963–1964. Photo by Thomas W. Fennell.

Pima, Northern and Southern Tepehuán, Tarahumara, Guarijío, Cora, and Huichol. All these groups
speak Uto-Aztecan languages, live in rancheria settlements, share a common material culture, and have
religious ceremonies centered around corn beer or
fruit wine. Probably all used Peyote in ceremonies.
Their subsistence strategy was hunting, wild gathering, and agriculture. This grouping has been called
the Northwest Mexican Ranchería culture area.

However, the model for St. John's Indian dancers
and drum and bugle corps was the Plains Indians.
For most of the public, they were the default Native
Americans. And they were what Michael drew.

In high school Michael cut hair in the boys' dor-
mitory to earn pocket money. When he graduated,
he went to barbers' school in Phoenix, Arizona. At
the nearby beautician school, he met a young Navajo
woman and married her at St. Mary's Roman Catholic Basilica in Phoenix. They had two children,
Michelle and Michael Jr. A third child, Christopher,
died in infancy.

Michael's first job out of barbers' school was in a
shop in Sunnyslope, a community in Phoenix. He
intended barbering to be his profession, but the Vietnam War changed his plans. The draft refused him
because of an ear condition, so he enlisted in the U.S.
Marine Corps. They were less fussy and sent him off
first to San Diego and then to Camp Pendleton Marine Corps Base for training. He
was the third member of his immediate family to become a Marine. He volunteered
for Vietnam "because I wanted to see everything."

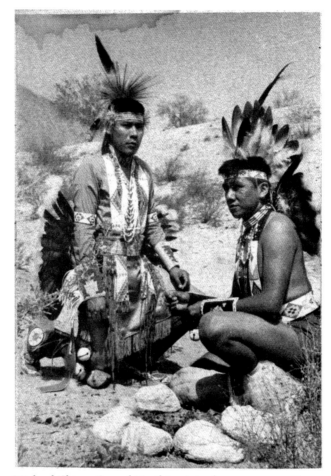

Michael Chiago Sr. and Virgil Lewis in dance costume. Photo
by Thomas W. Fennell (from an undated promotional magazine from St. John's Indian School).

Michael shipped out in 1968 and ran into several other St. John's graduates in
different platoons while he was overseas. He had finished the two-month training
for truck driving, but when the master sergeant saw on his résumé that he was
a licensed barber, Michael was told that's what he would be doing instead. He
rebelled, saying that he had come to fight, not to cut hair. He had to be sternly
reminded that in the military you follow orders, and the orders were that he was
to cut hair for the platoon.

The front lines saw the ugly face of war, but the platoon carpenters built him a
small shop and improvised a wooden barber's chair for him. Michael found a spent
mortar shell and painted red-and-white lines on it to advertise his activity. Men

came in with so much dirt or mud in their hair, Michael could scarcely cut it. Sometimes he had to resort to hand shears.

After six months in Vietnam, Michael returned to Arizona, his tour of duty finished. He was out of the Marines later in 1968 and did not reenlist. "Everything was just blank, my mind. I didn't do much," he said of this time period. Things did not go well on the home front, and he and his wife went their separate ways. Michael continued to support his two children, and for seven years he also helped raise two of his godchildren. It is the O'odham way for a relative to take over when the biological parents are having difficulties.

With his GI Bill benefits, Michael attended Maricopa Community College, then called Maricopa Technical College, in Phoenix, taking a program in commercial art studies and specializing in advertising. His first job was doing layout design for *Arizona Farmer-Ranchman* magazine. He did magazine design for the next three and a half years.

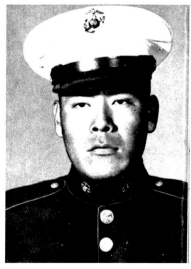

Michael in the Marine Corps, 1966. Photographer unknown.

ACHIEVING RECOGNITION AS AN ARTIST

Meanwhile, Michael was doing his own artwork, selling small pieces that featured fancy dancers, mostly with colored pencils and shading—no watercolors yet, though he made the switch by 1968. There were many Native American artists on the scene at the time, especially Hopi and Navajo. Harrison Begay, for instance, was a well-known contemporary. Michael's clientele was small, though he did sell some work through the Dundee, New York, shop of Thomas W. Fennell, a teacher at St. John's Indian School.

In 1971 Michael decided to try making a living as a fine artist. "I almost quit several times because I was bringing very little home, and I wasn't selling a lot, maybe thirty dollars a week. It took five years to really move art." He sold small paintings to the Gila River Indian Arts and Crafts Center, a tribal enterprise, for fifteen dollars each. Sometimes, he said, he would sit out in the car and have someone else take paintings in to show for possible gallery purchase so he wouldn't have to face rejection personally.

The Anasazi Gallery in Flagstaff, Arizona, picked up his work. They arranged his first television interview and also featured him in art demonstrations that they sponsored in Colorado, Virginia, and Arizona. Mike had to get used to being in the public eye, which he now enjoys.

Around 1975 business started to pick up, though his subject matter was still mostly Plains Indians and the occasional Pueblo kachina. "I painted fancy dancers because I knew that. I was an Indian dancer." Many other Native artists were doing

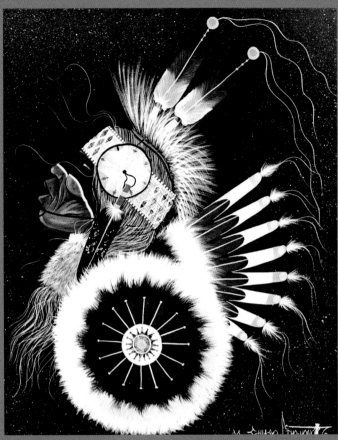

Michael's early paintings depicted traditional subjects. A fancy dancer is shown in this 1976 work. Photo by Thomas W. Fennell.

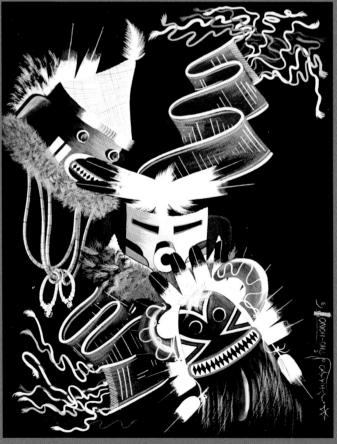

Another example of Michael's early work, from 1979, shows Hopi kachina masks. Photo by Thomas W. Fennell.

the same. One day someone looking at his work asked, "Why don't you paint your own people?" Mike thought about that. "It never occurred to me that someday I'd be doing my own people. So I started."

"I did basket weaving and pottery paintings for around twenty years, then I started doing art of everyday life." (This early focus on O'odham ceramics and basketry can occasionally be seen in some of his more recent work as well.)

In May 1980 *Arizona Highways* magazine published a special issue on solar energy. It included Michael's commissioned painting called *The Sun Supplies All Life*. "We need the sun for everyday life," he said of the painting. It depicted a rain dance with a *maakai* (shaman) leading. That year marked the beginning of a successful career doing O'odham paintings.

Examples of promotional posters painted by Michael Chiago Sr. Photos by Michelle Chiago.

An *Arizona Highways* cover painting in April 1999 further boosted interest in his work. It accompanied a story on the origin of the Saguaro cactus as recounted in an O'odham folktale. The editors of the magazine wrote him that it was their best-selling issue to date. (The magazine had started in the 1920s.)

Michael also did paintings to be reproduced on posters announcing events; this generated very little cash but brought Michael more into the public eye. Beginning in 1985 he provided the posters for O'odham Tash, an Indian festival, in Casa Grande, Arizona. Over the years he would do nine posters for this celebration. His 1990 poster *Circles of Friendship* was for the 32nd Annual Heard Museum Guild Indian Fair & Market, and he did the 2007 poster for the Pueblo Grande Museum Auxiliary Indian Market, both events in Phoenix.

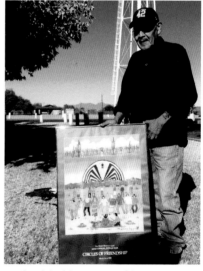

Michael holding one of his posters at Salt River. Photo by Michelle Chiago.

In 1996 the Heard Museum mounted a traveling exhibition called *Rain*, featuring how different southwestern groups depicted this life-giving resource. It went to the Museum of Mankind in London where Michael was artist-in-residence for two weeks. His two-piece acrylic painting was the largest piece in the exhibition, which then went to the Mashantucket Pequot Museum and Research Center in Connecticut, where Michael was featured for two days, before it came back to Heard Museum in Phoenix.

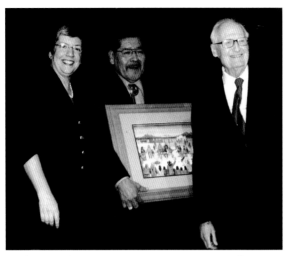

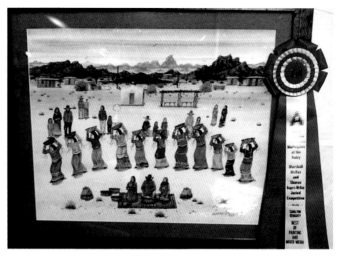

Michael and Arizona Governor Janet Napolitano at an awards ceremony, 2005. Photographer unknown.

A Chiago painting wins first place at the Gene Autry American Indian Market, 2013. Photo by Michelle Chiago.

In 2006 Michael was awarded the prestigious Arizona Indian Living Treasures Award. This lifetime award honors outstanding Native Americans for their contributions to traditional arts, education, cultural preservation, and language preservation.

Later, in the fall of 2012, his work was displayed in an invitation-only art exhibition in Paris, France, at the Grand Palais. This was the second exhibition of Native American and First Nations artists to be held in the Salon du Dessin et de la Peinture à l'Eau. He was featured along with eleven other Indigenous artists from the United States and Canada. Mike was the only representative from the Southwest.

Michael was well aware of the different schools of Native American art that were emerging throughout his career, beginning in the early seventies. *Arizona Highways* and other sources were

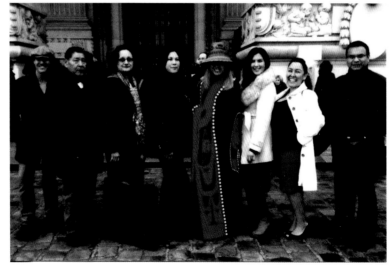

Michael, second from left, with seven of the other invited Native American and First Nations artists in Paris, 2012. Photo by Michelle Chiago.

featuring artists trained at the Institute of American Indian Arts (IAIA) in Santa Fe, New Mexico. The style was flat and stylized, predominantly Puebloan and Plains. Pablita Velarde of Santa Clara Pueblo is a prominent example of this school. Then Fritz Scholder, T. C. Cannon, Kevin Red Star, Sherman Chaddlesone, Stephen

Mopope, and others broke from that mold and began an entirely different, more abstract style with oil and acrylic portraits in bold colors. Powerful individuals emerged from their canvases. The movement was labeled "contemporary Native American art." Around the same time, Navajo artist R. C. Gorman took his inspiration from Costa Rican–born Mexican sculptor Francisco Zúñiga—Gorman's women are iconic—and the non-Native Tucsonan Ted de Grazia, the darling of *Arizona Highways*, was painting youthful Indians and swirling angels with rotund blank faces. It was a fertile period for the fine arts.

Instead, Michael, a self-taught artist, went his own way. For him, his local desert environment and quiet villages are his teachers: "I wanted to develop my own style, what I wanted to change. I look at desert scenes at different times of the day, throughout the day, how the sun changes the shadows. I try to develop what I see with my own eyes. I just do it in my head. I've seen a lot of good artists, but I do what I know on the desert. Sometimes I'll stop and examine a prickly-pear, how they grow, come out of the ground, how the spines are. Or I look at the Saguaro, how the shadows are, what the colors are. Or I go to the mountains and look at the petroglyphs, to look at the designs and re-create them in my painting."

There is a definite time frame to Michael's paintings. Most scenes are from his parents' and grandparents' time, much as ethnographer Ruth Underhill would have observed them during the days she worked among the O'odham in the 1930s and early 1940s. Many activities in the paintings, however, could just as well be contemporary. Men's outfits today are still mostly Western, while older women dress largely as Michael has painted them. When he was small, Michael noted that many O'odham women would buy commercial fabrics, cut the material, and sew their own dresses by hand; they had no sewing machines. For fiestas, they would buy bright colors—one color for the skirt, another for the blouse. But the scarves they would buy in stores. For ordinary days, they chose more muted colors.

These Desert People have watched the world change around them; they pick and choose what they may want to include in their lives, rejecting the rest. Most still speak their own language. The Tohono O'odham may keep their traditional medical practices with the *mamakai* (shamans), while also taking advantage of modern public health practices.

Many of Michael's paintings are based on conversations with his mother, aunts, and grandmother, in addition to his own daily experience. A painting may require extensive research; they are painstakingly accurate. He tells of driving out to east Tucson to interview the late Julian Hayden who watched the Navijhu and Wiigida ceremonies at Kaij Mek (Santa Rosa) in 1936 and 1945. Michael used the details that appeared in a special issue of the *Journal of the Southwest* (1987) but still went to talk with Hayden personally.

The brilliant desert is omnipresent. There are vast vistas in the paintings. This is the Basin and Range Province: Rugged mountains thrust up out of a sea of alluvium millions of years old. Every peak and range has its O'odham name. The vegetation is that of the Sonoran Desert with its characteristic Saguaros. This is Michael's lived environment.

Light is so important in this environment. Some paintings show people out in the cool morning hours before the desert heats up. But by ten on summer mornings, it's time to retire to the shade of the *watto* (*vatto*), 'an outdoor arbor'. This is the time and place for other activities. Other paintings show evening scenes with their spectacular sunsets; some are nighttime scenes. O'odham are an outdoor people; relatively few of Michael's paintings show indoor activities such as the diagnosing and curing sessions.

A stylistic progression is evident throughout the decades that Michael has been painting Native life. Earlier paintings are somewhat more stylized, a token to the IAIA school (see, for instance, his Navijhu painting done in 1983—note the mid-ground compared to the same ceremony created in 2021 on page 82). He eventually abandoned even this concession to the IAIA school. There was also a period

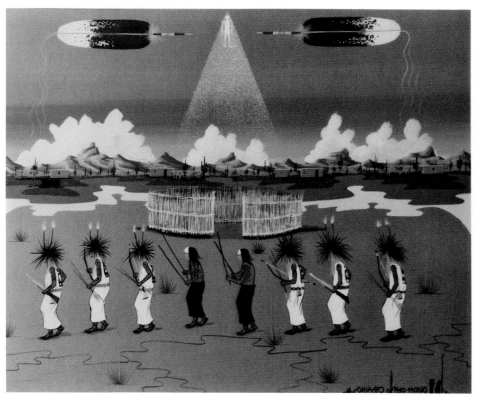

Michael's stylized 1983 painting of Nanavajhu dancers and attendants. Painting and photo courtesy of Wade C. Sherbrooke.

of about five years in which Michael struggled to see details due to bad cataracts, though he has said his work from the last ten years, after he had corrective eye surgery, feels more accurate.

Michael has a distinctive palette and has used the same watercolors—Grumbacher Academy—since 1971; they give him the transparency he wants and, when mixed with white, the right opacity. Throughout much of the day the tone of the desert is flat, but at daybreak and again around sunset, the desert is brilliantly colored. And this is the light that Michael usually captures in his paintings. We see it also in the clothing of the O'odham. His figures manifest subtle reminders of Georges Rouault, another narrative painter who found his own way. For larger projects, such as murals, Michael uses acrylics. He keeps all his brushes; sometimes the older ones are more responsive to his needs.

Sometimes Michael paints himself into the picture as the hatless little boy in a blue shirt. He is on the sidelines, taking it all in. He is observing the activities, learning the culture, the inquisitive Native ethnographer.

Michael also collaborated on a children's book, *Sing Down the Rain* (1997). Judi Moreillon wrote the text, which is actually a poem that can be performed as a choral reading. It is illustrated with a dozen of Michael's paintings, has gone through four printings, and is about to be reissued by a different press. His artwork additionally adorns the covers of several University of Arizona Press books.

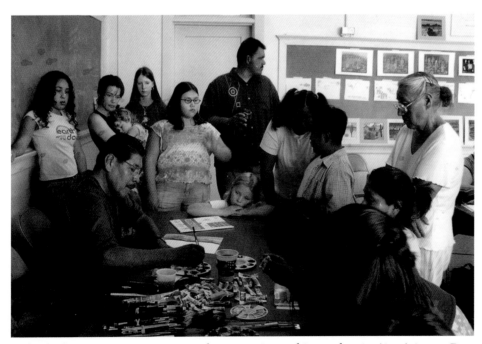

Michael Chiago Sr. giving a painting demonstration to his art class in Ajo, Arizona. Date and photographer unknown.

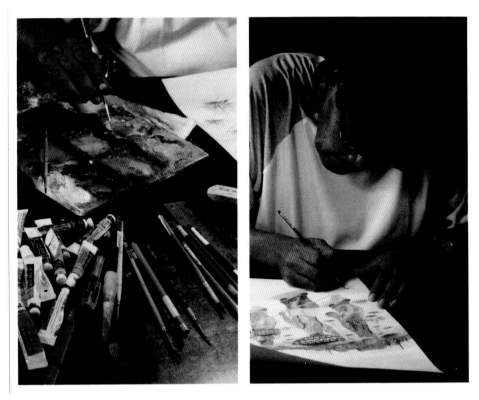

The artist in his home studio, 1995. Photo by Susan Randall, courtesy of the *Casa Grande Dispatch*.

PUBLIC ART

Various pieces of public art by Michael Chiago Sr. can be seen throughout Arizona. A large painting hangs in Phoenix's Sky Harbor Airport. Another can be found at Casa Grande Ruins National Monument near Coolidge, Arizona. A wall painting graces the Basha's grocery store in Sells, Arizona, the headquarters for the Tohono O'odham tribe. A very large mural is on the wall of a public building in Ajo, Arizona. Michael also painted a two-story-high telescope part at Kitt Peak National Observatory on the main Tohono O'odham reservation. The subject of all these is O'odham life.

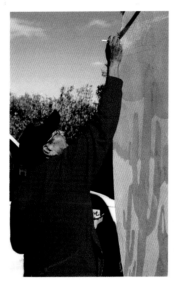
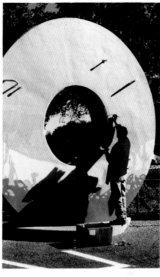

Michael Chiago Sr. begins painting a mural on a copy of a telescope part at Kitt Peak National Observatory on the Tohono O'odham Reservation, Arizona, 2006.

Completed mural at Kitt Peak National Observatory.

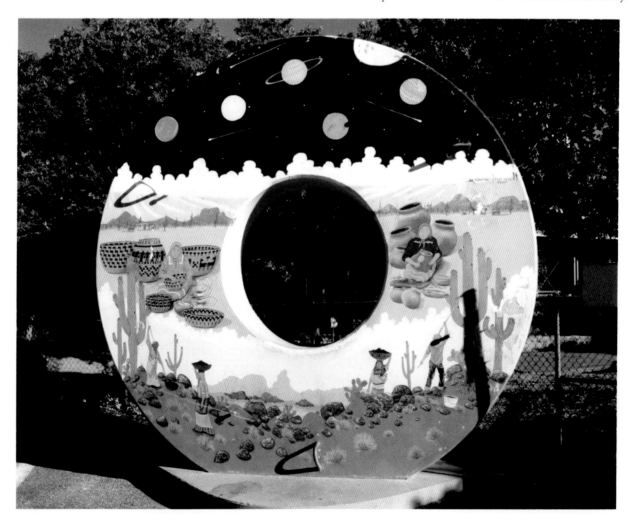

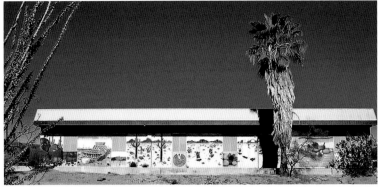

Michael Chiago murals on a public building in Ajo, Arizona. Photo by Michelle Chiago.

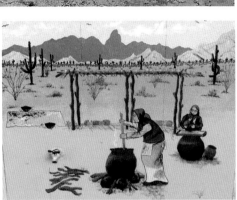

Details of Ajo mural. Photos by Wade C. Sherbrooke.

Chiago mural on Basha's Grocery, Sells, Arizona. Photo by Michelle Chiago.

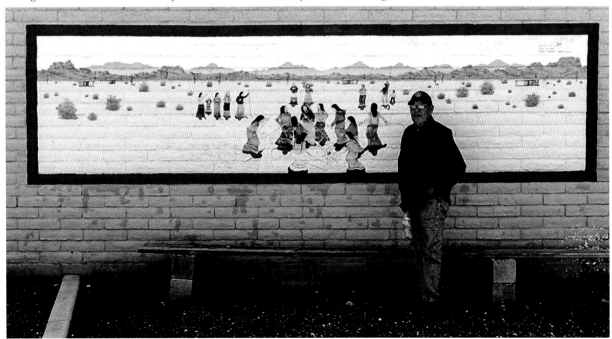

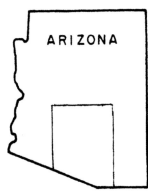

ARIZONA

MAP OF PIMAN RESERVATIONS
AND LOCALES CITED

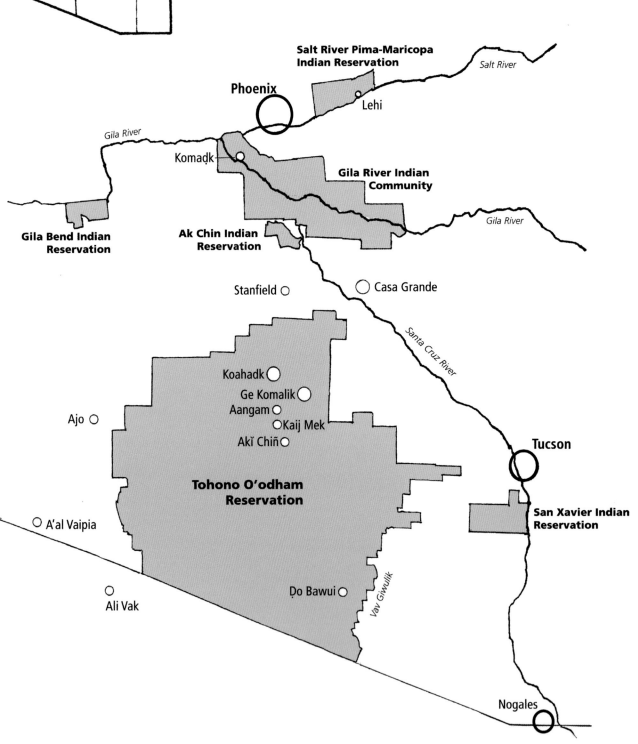

Salt River Pima-Maricopa
Indian Reservation

Salt River

Phoenix

Lehi

Gila River

Komaḍk

Gila River Indian
Community

Gila River

Gila Bend Indian
Reservation

Ak Chin Indian
Reservation

Stanfield

Casa Grande

Santa Cruz River

Koahadk

Ge Komalik

Aangam

Kaij Mek

Ajo

Akǐ Chiñ

Tohono O'odham
Reservation

Tucson

San Xavier Indian
Reservation

A'al Vaipia

Ali Vak

Ḍo Bawui

Vav Giwulik

Nogales

1

ENVIRONMENTAL SETTING

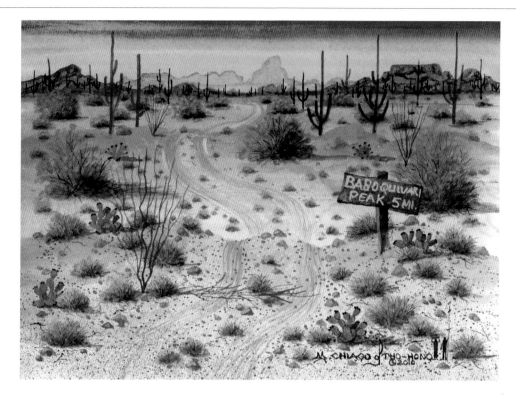

O'ODHAM COUNTRY

The Upper Pimans live in the Sonoran Desert of southern Arizona and northern Sonora, Mexico. Those who occupy what is called the Arizona Uplands of the Sonoran Desert are mostly referred to as Tohono O'odham, Desert People. Those who live along permanent desert streams and rivers, such as the Gila and Lower Salt Rivers, are called the Akimel O'odham, River People. In this painting, as in most, Michael shows the Arizona Uplands. There are other lowland Pimans, the Pima Bajo of Sonora, who call themselves O'odaam. None of Michael's paintings depict these people of the thornscrub and tropical deciduous forest country.

At first the desert appears barren and unproductive, but here we see a landscape covered with diverse vegetation. Different seasons bring different wild crops. On close look, we see one plant species awaiting harvest.

Much of O'odham country is traversed via dirt roads by the lonely horseman, wagon, or pickup. This particular road leads to Baboquivari Peak in a prominent mountain range formed by the Quinlan Mountains in the north, Baboquivari Mountains in the middle, and Pozo Verde Mountains in the south. Together they form a conspicuous segment of the horizon southwest of Tucson. The painting, however, shows the range looking eastward from the O'odham homeland.

The name Baboquivari comes from the early Spanish attempt to render the O'odham name of the most prominent peak, *waw* or *vav*, 'cliff or outcrop', and *giwulikĭ*, 'constricted, belted, or cinched'. The peak rises almost 8,000 feet above sea level. At its base is a cave, one of the homes of O'odham culture hero I'itoi or Se'ehe. (He has other homes in the volcanic Pinacate Peaks and in the South Mountains near Laveen, Arizona; his fourth home seems to have been forgotten.) Offerings accompanying petitions are still made at all three places, but the Baboquivari location is the most important in modern Tohono O'odham thought.

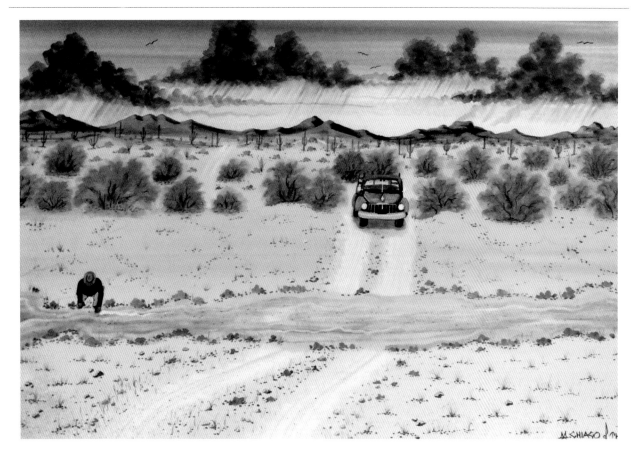

FLASH FLOODS IN THE DESERT

Sudden summer storms can drop an enormous amount of *juukĭ*, 'rain', in a very short time. Some of the water soaks into the thirsty desert soil, but much of it collects in the *a'akĭ*, 'arroyos or washes', filling them to their banks, turning them into muddy, detritus-filled torrents. The storm itself may be far away and out of sight, but here we see it falling on the distant mountains. The flood may subside almost as quickly as it started.

Many unwary travelers have been victims of these flash floods. In the early 1900s Indian photographer Edward S. Curtis lost a wagon and many of his Tohono O'odham photographs while traveling in their home-lands. Father Bonaventure Oblasser photographed his stranded open vehicle being towed by a wagon and team of horses. A man at Quitovac oasis, where the Wiigida is still carried out, publicly scoffed at the effectiveness of the August ceremony to bring the summer rains. He left, riding into the east, before the ritual was competed. On his way back to his home village, he had to cross a large wash where he was overtaken by a flash flood. They eventually found his dead horse far downstream.

In this painting a man has stopped his pickup at a small *akĭ* and is testing the depth of the water with a stick to see if he can safely cross. He knows the ways of the desert.

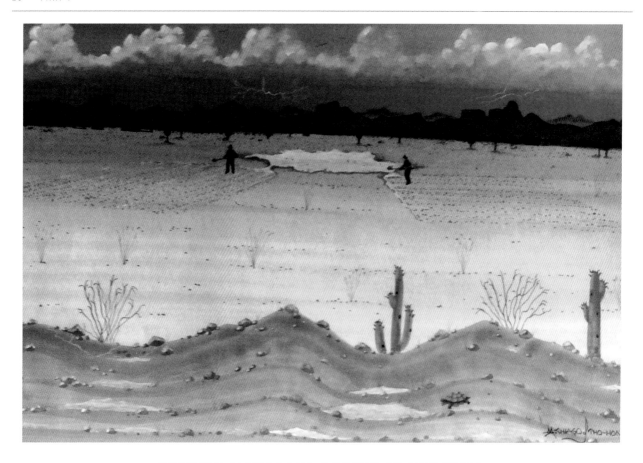

SUMMER MONSOONS ARRIVE AT THE WO'O

If the O'odham have carried out their sacred wine feast to call the clouds, they will come up out of the east or southeast, dropping their precious moisture on the desert. Still the singing will continue to entice the storms as at least another good rain will be necessary to produce a crop.

This painting captures the darkness of a ferocious rainstorm over the desert. Water has already filled their *wo'o* (*vo'o*), 'charco', a water catchment pond on the desert floor. The farmers are spreading the impounded rainwater on their fields. Some O'odham also make a *wachkĭ* (*vachkĭ*), or small pond near their house for domestic water.

The crops are fast-maturing varieties that have been selected over generations for desert farming: *bawĭ* (*bavĭ*), 'teparies', a species of bean that can produce four times as much seed on a quarter the amount of the water that it would take *muuñ*, common beans such as pintos, to mature; a variety of *huuñ*, 'maize or corn', with small stalks and leaves that yields medium-sized ears a month quicker than most other strains; *toki*, a cotton cultivar that matures in 150 days rather than 180 days; and *haal*, a species of squash that is at home in the hot, dry heat. In addition, there were *kovĭ*, domesticated forms of chenopods, and *giad*, domesticated forms of amaranths, that grew like weeds, producing prodigious amounts of protein-rich seeds. These are all warm-season crops. After the arrival of the Spanish, other crops such as *pilkañ*, 'wheat', were planted in winter, and *miiloñ*, 'melons', and *gepĭ*, 'watermelons', in summer.

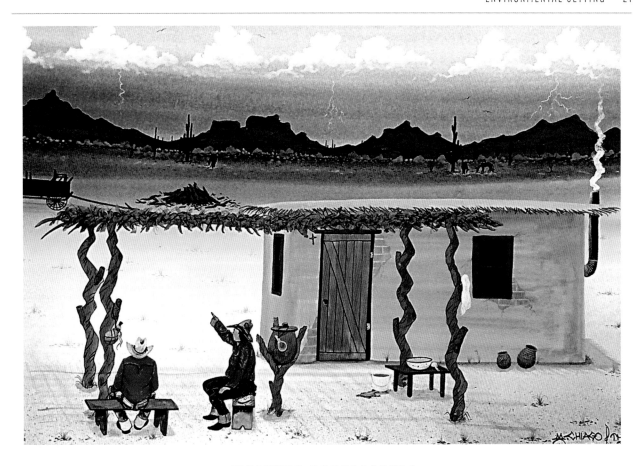

WEATHER FORECASTERS

Like farmers everywhere, the O'odham paid close attention to the weather, especially the life-bringing rains. In the wide-open country of the Sonoran Desert, storms are often dramatic. Lighter rains from the Pacific come from the west in the winter, while heavier rains from tropical storms or monsoons come in the summer from the east or southeast. The aboriginal crops of amaranth, goosefoot, pumpkins, squash, teparies, and maize were warm-season crops growing in the monsoon season. Spaniards introduced winter crops such as barley, wheat, lentils, and chickpeas. Additionally, various wild greens flourished with the winter rains, while other species grew in the summer, often alongside planted crops.

As to be expected, the O'odham developed a complex vocabulary for meteorological phenomena. The general term for rain is *juukĭ*, while clouds are *chevagĭ*, and wind is *hewel* (*hevel*). Rains from the gentler winter storms are called *hikshpi juukĭ*, a term that can be used for light rains at other seasons as well. A fine, misty rain is *shu'uwaḍ juukĭ* because the drops are like the tiny seeds of the Tansy-mustard.[1] But strong winter rains whipped back and forth by the north wind are *wamaḍ juukĭ* named after the racer, a very long and active snake well-known to the O'odham. In the summer, a monsoon downpour is sometimes preceded by a violent dust

---

1. Out of respect for nonhuman life, the terminal names for both plants and animals have been treated as proper nouns.

storm called *jegos* (see page 39). *Siw hewel* (*siv hevel*), 'stern wind', is a microburst. One word, *gew* (*gev*) labels both snow and ice. Hail is *chea* or *chia*.

Red lightning that passes from one cloud to another is *wepegi*. (The word is also used today for electricity.) Lightning that strikes the ground or some object is *wuihomĭ*. Like the wind, this lightning is personified in folktales and culture. Anything that Wuihomĭ has claimed as his own, such as a tree, must be avoided for fear of contracting *O'odham mumkidag* or *kaachim mumkidag*, 'staying sickness'. The same is true of any Saguaro or tree that a *hikwig* (*hikvig*), or Gila Woodpecker, has appropriated for its nest hole. Thunder is *tatañikĭ*.

In one O'odham folktale, Juukĭ is blind and must be led by Hevel. So the wind always precedes the rain storm, especially the heavy ones of summer.

Certain *mamakai* might be specialists in bringing rain. Most O'odham ceremonies ultimately had to do with rain petitions, but the most important invocation for rains is the midsummer Saguaro wine feast.

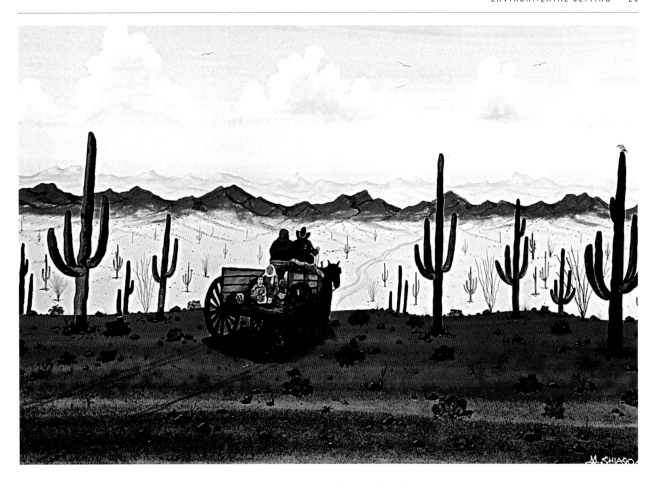

RESERVATION ROADS

Many O'odham villages in the vast Pimería Alta are connected only by dirt roads, passable when conditions are suitable. Only in the last forty or fifty years have many roads been paved.

When the artist's mother was due with him, his parents loaded the wagon at Lehi on the Salt River Pima–Maricopa Indian Community near Scottsdale, Arizona, and headed for the Koahadk village on the main Tohono O'odham Reservation. His mother knew there was a good midwife there. The trip took two days, passing through the Gila River Indian Community.

Michael confesses that he doesn't remember a lot of details of this arduous trip he painted except that they made it on time, and then they returned to Salt River. Years later his mother would point out the spot in the Sacaton Mountains near the modern freeway where they camped overnight with their new baby.

DESERT OASES

Water is the limiting factor for human life in the desert. Tohono O'odham were once a two-village people. In the summer, water could be impounded from storm runoff for domestic use and for farming small fields in the lowlands. At dawn, women and girls might walk miles to get water for the day's use. When these sources dried, the people moved back to their winter villages in the mountains where there were springs. Plunge pools, called *chechpo* (sing., *cheepo*) or *tinajas* in Spanish, might capture large quantities of water in mountain ranges such as the Tinajas Altas.

In a few places, such as Quitovac and Quitobaquito, there are oases, ponds of spring-fed surface water in the desert. The one shown here was once home for a few O'odham families. They were evacuated with the formation of Organ Pipe Cactus National Monument and evidence of their former occupation obliterated. The government concept of pristine environment does not acknowledge the human occupation of these water holes for ten thousand years or more. Scientists studying this park service oasis and another south of the border still occupied by O'odham found greater biological diversity and individual numbers of plants and animals (overall biomass) at the Native American–managed oasis.

The cactus in this painting are *chuchuis*, or Organ Pipe Cactus, smaller than the *haashañ*, or Saguaro, and with more arms. On one is perched a *haupal*, or Red-tailed Hawk, on another a *kuukvul*, or Western Screech-Owl, with a small woodpecker, perhaps a *hikwig* (*hikvig*) or *chehegam*, in the middle. Several *vachpik*, 'coots', swim in the oasis.

In contrast, the Akimel O'odham were called one-village people because they did not have to move seasonally in search of water. They farmed the banks of desert streams with permanent flow: the Gila, the Upper Santa Cruz, and the San Pedro. On the Gila, they farmed both the banks and the islands—the spring snow melt in the uplands and the rise of the river from the summer rainstorms in the eastern mountains allowed growing two crops consecutively in one long, frost-free season.

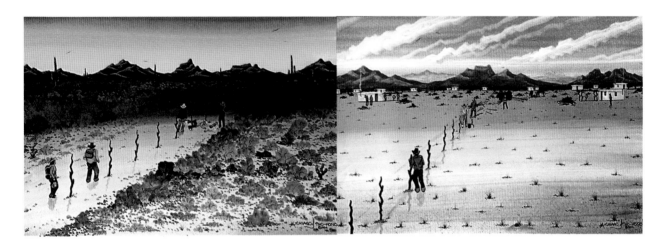

INTERNATIONAL BORDER

With the Treaty of Guadalupe Hidalgo in 1848, the Gila River divided the United States from Mexico. Until the Gadsden Purchase in 1854, both Tohono and Akimel O'odham interacted with Sonora, Mexico, as the colonial government, as even the Akimel O'odham, living primarily on the south bank of the Gila, were in Mexico. The new international boundary changed all of this.

As it did with several other Indigenous groups, the boundary survey cut through tribal holdings, leaving villages on either side of the line. Now some Tohono O'odham were in Sonora, but more were in Arizona. They continued to interact locally, but most Upper Pimans lost contact with their immediate cousins, the Pima Bajo, farther south in Sonora.

The boundary has caused many problems for the Tohono O'odham. Their southern border shares 70 miles with Sonora. Access to religious ceremonies in the south, such as at Magdalena de Kino and Quitovac, has been complicated by government paperwork. Undocumented migrants have flooded across tribal lands. The safety of villagers is sometimes compromised. Drug trafficking is a reality. The ubiquitous presence of the U.S. Border Patrol has been an imposition on a quiet way of life.

2

SUBSISTENCE ACTIVITIES

Wild Harvest

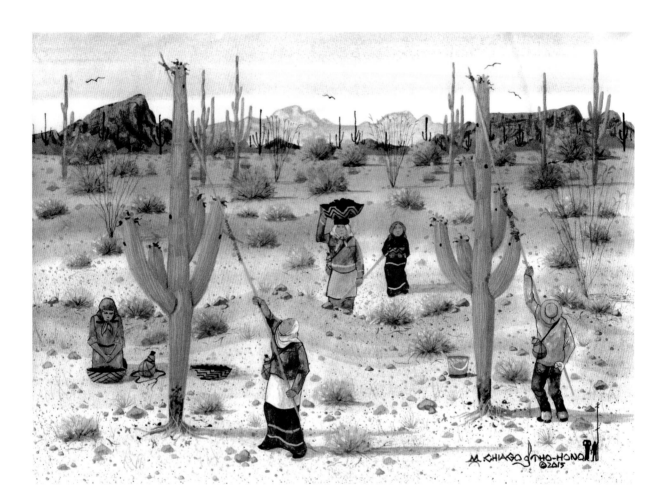

THE SAGUARO HARVEST

The *haashañ*, the Saguaro cactus, is iconic of the Sonoran Desert and plays a significant role in the economic life of the Desert People. Not surprisingly, Saguaro camp activities are a frequent subject of Michael Chiago Sr.'s paintings.

The O'odham new year begins with the Saguaro harvest in late June through early July. This is called *haashañ bahidag mashad*, 'Saguaro fruit moon or month'. At that time, many O'odham families go to their traditional family harvest camps for several weeks. The Saguaros grow best on the well-drained bajadas skirting the rocky desert ranges. Women, men, and children all work hard in the cool mornings before the midday temperatures soar to 110 degrees and above. The *haashañ* bloom sequentially, so the ripening extends over two or three weeks.

The *bahidag*, or fruit, still atop the cactus is knocked down with a *ku'ibaḍ*. This picking tool is made of several *waapai* (*vaapai*), 'Saguaro ribs', lashed end to end. The *waapai*, taken from a dead and decayed cactus, are light but surprisingly strong. A crosspiece, called the *matsig* or *machchuḍ*, is tied at an angle to the main pole. The *ku'ibaḍ* either pushes the fruit up with the smaller angle or hooks the fruit down with its opposite side. The fallen fruit are then gathered into *wapaldi*, 'buckets', or *hohoa*, 'large tray baskets'. Michael has shown some of the *kuku'ibaḍ* with a crossbar halfway down the shaft. This is to dislodge fruit from the lower Saguaro side arms, called *mamhaḍag*.

Now *eḍaj*, the sweet, juicy red pulp, is pushed out of its tough greenish or reddish rind using a finger or thumb. But the rinds are not cast off carelessly. Their inside walls are bright crimson, so they are carefully placed on the ground, red side skyward as a votive prayer for rain. Cactus camp is in the pre-monsoon season, and all the activities are in anticipation of the summer rains.

A sweet drink called *ia vaḍagĭ* is made by mixing water with the fruit. The juicy pulp itself, *ia*, is filled with small black seeds, the *kaij*. These are a rich source of proteins and fats.

Some of the fruit pulp dries, either up on the cactus or fallen around the base; this is called *gakidag*. One woman is shown on her knees gathering the *gakidag* that's fallen from the cactus; it can be pressed into a cake called *juñ* that keeps indefinitely. Pieces of *juñ* may be broken off and added to any dish that needs sweetening, such as *haakĭ chu'i*, or just eaten like candy, seeds and all.

Michael also has shown the pickers with gourd canteens. The *wako* (*vako*) is light and more durable than the heavy *ha'a*, 'water ollas', which will be used back at camp to boil down the *bahidag* into *sitol*, 'syrup'. The black opening he has painted on some saguaro is the *haashañ shuud* or *hikvig kii*, the nest hole made by either the Gila Woodpecker or Gilded Flicker. They, too, enjoy the juicy fruits.

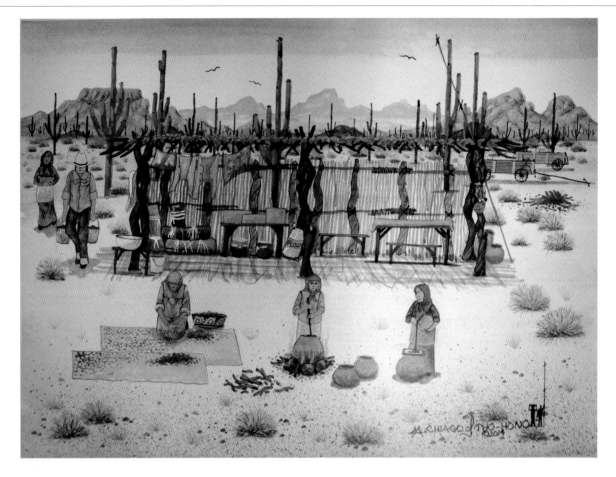

SAGUARO CAMP

An extended family or several families maintain traditionally held camps where they go for several weeks to harvest cactus fruit. A large *watto* (*vatto*), an open arbor or ramada, provides shade in the hot June or early July sun.

After picking Saguaro fruits during the cool hours of dawn, everyone converges back at the Saguaro camp for the late morning and afternoon work.

Here is bedding carefully rolled up and stashed against the back wall of Ocotillo stalks. On the other side are the table and bench where the families eat. In the middle is a sack of *chu'i*, 'wheat flour', for making *chechemait*, 'tortillas', suspended from a *chettonḍag*, 'vertical support post', out of the way of hungry rodents.

A man returns from picking with two buckets full of juicy Saguaro fruit called *bahidaj*. The woman next to him probably carries a basketful of *gakidaj*, the already dried Saguaro fruit. A woman kneels on a canvas and separates the dried fruit from the hulls. She molds these into balls of sweet pulp with the seeds. In the center, another woman is stirring a batch of fresh fruit mixed with water, boiling it down. At right, a woman pours the cooked mass through the *o'osidakuḍ*, 'strainer'. The thick, dark red *sitol* collects in the *ha'a* below and is then kept in small jars. Some of it, diluted with water, is fermented to make *haashañ navait*, 'Saguaro wine', for the annual wine feast.

The *kaij* and stringy part of the pulp are strained out, then dried and cleaned or fed to the chickens. Like the *sitol*, the *kaij* have a long shelf life. When ready for use, they are ground on a *machchuḍ*, 'metate or grindstone', with whole wheat, then cooked to make a nutritious porridge called *ku'ul* or *haashañ kai hidoḍ*. This dish, rich in proteins and fats, was an important dietary item for both Tohono and Akimel O'odham.

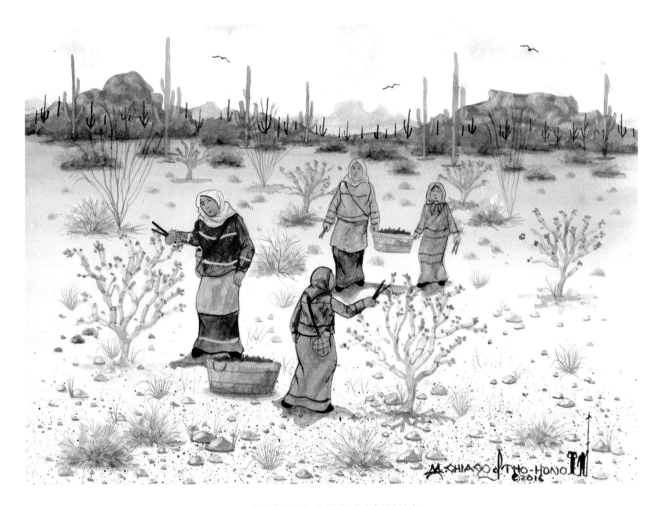

CHOLLA BUD PICKING

One of the staple foods of the O'odham was *hannam*, or *cheolim*, 'cholla buds', which appear on the cholla cactus each spring. The O'odham use several different species, all with different flowering times.

Picking begins in the cool morning hours and lasts until the desert starts to heat up. Using split-twig *waa'o* (*vaa'o*), 'tongs', the women twist off the unopened flower bud with the attached green fruit called *iibdaj*. Men come out to pick as well and help with the heavy lifting. Washtubs and five-gallon buckets are filled then packed down with a rock and filled with more buds. If the flowers are already opened, they cannot be used.

The buds may be roasted either out on the bajadas, or foothills, where the Chollas grow or taken back home. In either case, a *hannam chuamaikuḍ*, 'pit or ground oven', is dug and lined with rocks, then a fire is built in the pit, heating the rocks and earth. Firing to completely burn down the mesquite wood to coals and reach the right temperature may take around four hours. Then the pit is lined with fresh branches of *shegoi*, 'Creosote Bush', or succulent *chuchk onk*, 'Seepweed', so the delicate buds are not burned by the hot rocks.

Some women de-spine the buds before pit roasting, others after the buds have come out of the pit and dried. This involves sweeping the buds back and forth over a wire mesh, usually nailed to the bottom of a type of wooden frame called an *uso*. In either case, the raw buds are dumped into the pit and covered with more fresh branches, then an old hide, piece of burlap or canvas, or section of corrugated metal roofing. Finally a thick layer of dirt is shoveled over the top of the *hannam chuamaikuḍ* to hold in heat.

The pit is left to steam overnight, then checked around twelve hours later to see if the buds are cooked. If not, the pit is recovered and left until late afternoon. If still not done, the *hannam* can be boiled a few more hours on the stove. The cooked buds are spread out in the hot desert sun to dry completely.

Once dried, the *hannam* can be kept indefinitely in glass jars or clay ollas. When needed, it is rehydrated by boiling for a few hours. It can be served as is or cooked with onions or some kind of *iiwagĭ* (*iivagĭ*), 'wild greens'. This is how they usually appear at feast day celebrations. But the dried buds can also be ground and mixed with coarse whole wheat flour to make *atol* or *ku'ul*, 'gravy'.

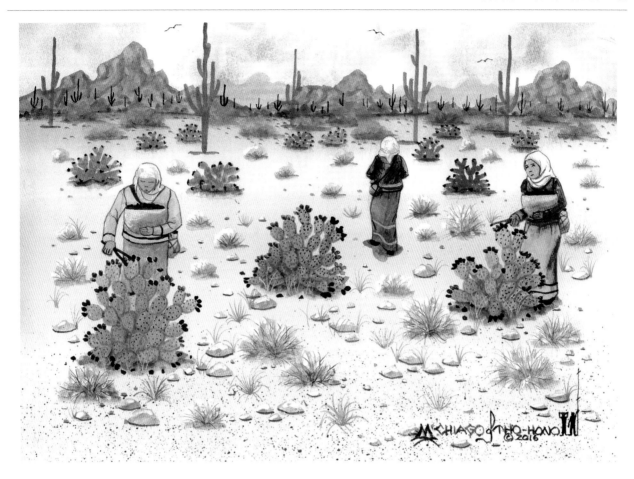

PICKING PRICKLY-PEAR FRUIT

The fruit of the *naw* (*nav*), 'prickly-pear cactus', ripens in summer or fall, depending on the species. When the *iibhai*, or fruit, are red and juicy, they are ready for harvest. The women pick the fruit with *waa'o* (*vaa'o*). Then they break branches off some small bush as Michael has shown growing here, and vigorously roll the fruit in the sand to remove the tiny *vii ho'i*, 'glochids'. Then the *iibhai* can be eaten as is or boiled down into a *sitol*. Like *haashañ sitol*, *iibhai sitol* can be kept for long periods sealed in small ollas or clay pots, but the sugar content must be high.

Some forms of the prickly-pear have fruit that can cause chills or lameness, so only a small amount can be eaten at once, perhaps two or three or maybe even four. Others have no effect. Fruit of the spineless domesticated prickly-pear, sometimes grown in Native gardens, does not have this consequence.

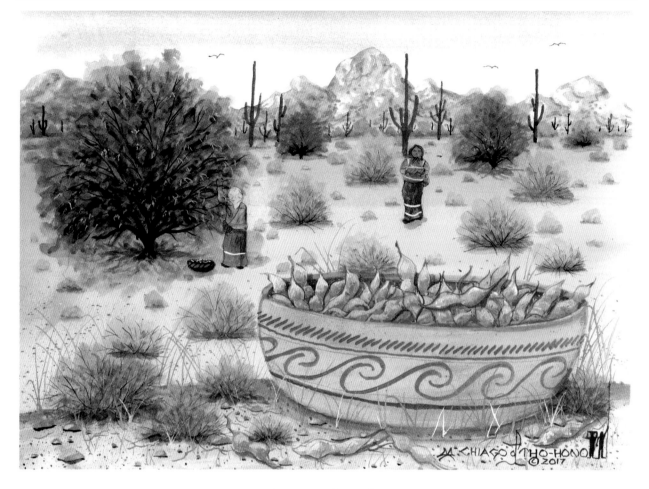

DESERT IRONWOOD

While the all-important *kui*, Velvet Mesquite, proliferates lower on the floodplains along streams and rivers, the Desert Ironwood prefers the drier bajadas that skirt the desert ranges. Here the trees grow mostly along the *a'aki*, giving them the appearance of dried-out creeks coming down the mountains. About the time the desert begins to be seriously hot in late May, many ironwoods are covered with clusters of pink or purple pea-like blossoms.

For the O'odham, this leguminous tree is called *ho'idkam,* meaning it has *ho'i*, 'thorns'. In late summer, the pods could be knocked down from a tree onto a canvas or picked up from the ground, then the hard outer husks could be crushed and the several large brown seeds removed. The seeds are soaked to remove bitterness, then dried and parched. They could be eaten as is or ground into meal.

The English name *ironwood* comes from the very dense, heavy, dark brown wood that could be made into tools almost as hard as iron. O'odham made their *giikĭ*, 'short digging hoe', from the wood; after the introduction of wheat and other European crops, they used the wood for the plow, also called a *giikĭ*. In the days of defensive warfare, the potato masher–style *shonchkĭ*, 'war club', might be made from ironwood or mesquite root, a very effective weapon in hand-to-hand combat.

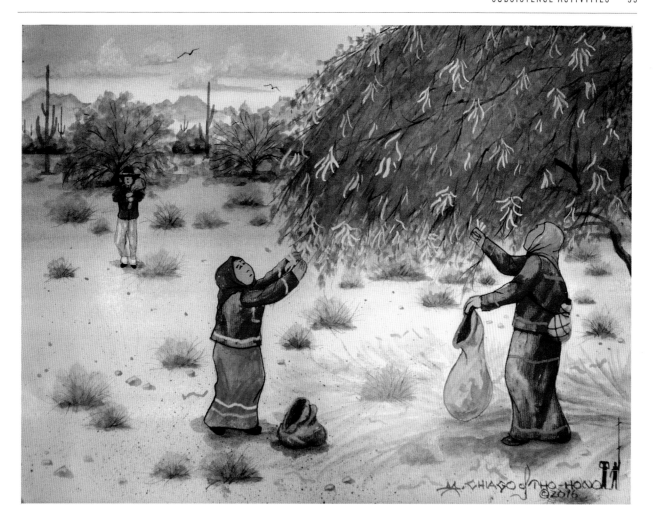

GATHERING MESQUITE PODS

Great bosques of *kui*, Velvet Mesquite, once lined the river bottoms of the major streams throughout the desert (the Gila, Santa Cruz, San Pedro, and Sonoyta Rivers). It also grew along *a'akĭ*, and even out on the plains, particularly after the introduction of grazing animals. The largest trees were in groves along the larger rivers.

One lunar month in spring was called *kui i'ivagĭdag mashad*, when the deciduous mesquite sprouts its fine leaves, followed by *kui hiosig mashad*, when the mesquite bursts out with abundant yellow flowers. When the mesquites leaf out, the O'odham knew that it was safe to plant their warm-season crops, as the mesquite always knows when the last of the killing frosts are over.

Once or sometimes twice a year, the trees produce a crop of long, beanlike pods, a primary food for Indians throughout the Sonoran Desert, as well as for many mammals. When the *wihog* (*vihog*), 'pods', mature and fall in the summer heat, the O'odham would drive their wagons into the *s-kuig* or *kui sha'ik*, 'bosque', and harvest pods by the ton, filling their gunnysacks and wagons. The pods contain a sweet, carbohydrate-rich pulp in which the very hard seeds are embedded. Soluble fiber in the *vihog* was a natural defense against diabetes.

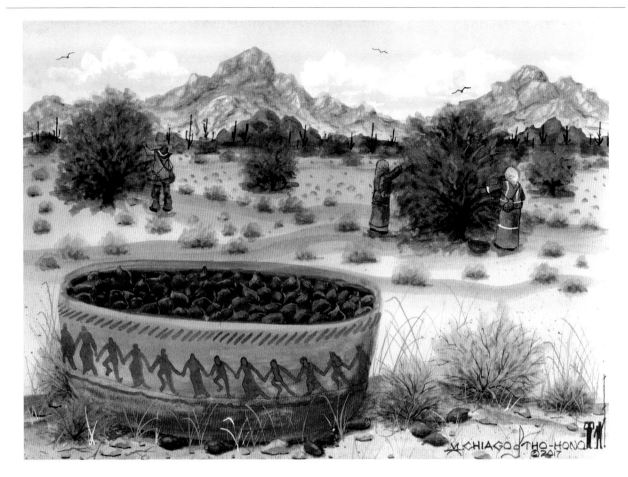

GATHERING ACORNS

Oak trees grow in several of the higher mountains that rise above the Saguaros and Sonoran Desert of Tohono O'odham country. The primary oak found here is the Emory Oak, but the Mexican Blue Oak grows here as well. Both are called *toa* in O'odham. Usually there is no separate word distinguishing the tree from the acorn as there is in some other languages. Tohono and Akimel O'odham often use the word *wiyóodi* (*viyóodi*), a loan word from Spanish *bellota*, 'acorn'. There also is a record of the oak tree being referred to as *wiyóodi je'ej*, 'acorn's mother'.

Western Apache still maintain acorn camps near the Arizona-Sonora border south of their current reservations. Tohono O'odham usually harvested in the foothills of the mountains closer to home. Acorns were among the trade items they took north to the Akimel O'odham at wheat harvest time. Today both groups obtain packets of acorns on their annual fall pilgrimage to Magdalena, Sonora.

Emory Oaks are most sought after because they have a good flavor and low tannin content. The acorns can be cracked and eaten raw without further preparation as a snack food, though formerly Tohono O'odham parched and ground the meats into meal, then cooked the *chu'i* into *ku'ul*, 'gravy', or an *atol*, 'porridge'.

Hunting

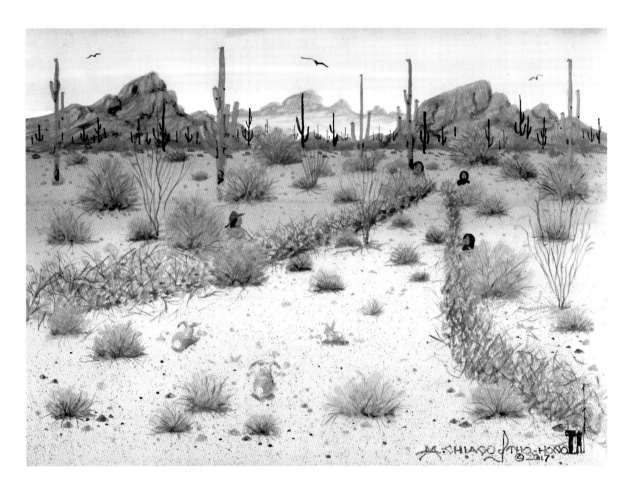

THE *SHAADA* OR COMMUNAL GAME DRIVE

When the *tobdam*, the village activity coordinator or hunt leader, announced there was going to be a *shaada*, 'rabbit hunt', all the men and boys of the village assembled at the designated place in the early dawn hours. The *tobdam* was the one who had memorized the formal oration that would initiate the surround. He used *s-moik ñe'okĭ* (also *ñi'okĭ*), 'soft talk', that referred to the game obliquely so as not to offend the animals that were to be hunted.

The goal was to sweep through the grassy and bushy country in one or two great arcs, running and shouting, beating the vegetation, and driving the game into a brush funnel, where hunters were waiting at the narrow end. With arrows and clubs, they dispatched the *totobĭ*, 'cottontails', and *chuuvĭ*, 'jackrabbits', the target game. If the growth was thick, *vopsho*, 'cotton rats', and *kokson*, 'pack rats', might be taken as well, some killed by the runners as they closed in. These were the four main meat sources for both Tohono and Akimel O'odham.

Older, less agile men waited near the narrow end where they gathered wood and prepared a hole to *chuama*, 'pit roast', the game, then everyone feasted. The extra meat was divided equally among all the participants— including those who had been less successful in the kill—to take home to their families.

Another kind of communal surround, called the *kuunama*, 'fire drive', was used in thick grassy areas or marshes and took much the same animals, but it was particularly successful with the *vopsho*, considered the prime game. (Solitary hunters, using a different strategy called *vipiamaḍ*, 'stalking', took *huawĭ* [*huai*], 'Mule Deer'; *siskĭ*, 'White-tailed Deer'; and *kukuvid*, 'Pronghorns'.)

In pre-cattle days, before overgrazing, the country supported a much heavier population of rodents, lagomorphs, and native ungulates. In 1539 Fray Marcos de Niza, traveling through northwest Mexico, wrote that local hunters could secure enough game for his retinue of around three hundred people in a matter of a few hours.

Agriculture

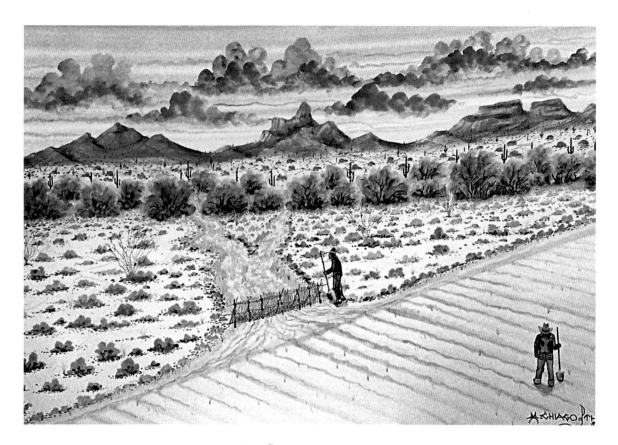

AK**Ɪ**CHI**Ñ** OR DRY FARMING

The O'odham—Akimel O'odham, Tohono O'odham, and Hia ch-eḍ O'odham—were excellent farmers in what appears to be a harsh environment. The Akimel O'odham relied on the twice annual rise in streams to flood their riverbank and island fields, first in the spring following snow melt in the distant uplands, then in midsummer with the monsoons falling in the local mountains. With fast-maturing crops, they could double-crop their fields.

The Tohono O'odham, who had no permanent streams on their land, relied on *akĭ chiñ*, 'flash-flood dry farming'. Summer rains falling on the desert mountains collected in *a'akĭ*. As the water rushed down the bajadas skirting the base of the mountains, it slowed down and spread out at the *chiñ*, 'mouth', of the *akĭ*. Here the flow dropped its rich load of animal droppings, particularly from cottontails and jackrabbits, and leaflets from leguminous trees such as ironwood, paloverdes, and mesquites on the bajadas. So precious was this nitrogen-rich detritus that the O'odham had a special name for it—*wakola* (*vakola*)—and even sang songs praising it.

The desert farmer plowed the alluvial fan at the bottom, even constructing small check dams to slow the water, ensuring that it would soak deeply into the rich *akĭ chiñ* soil. A *komkĭchud*, 'Desert Tortoise', leaves its cool burrow to tank up on fresh rainwater.

The thunderheads over the eastern horizon are flashing with lightning and have begun to drop their moisture load on the mountains. Cloud bursts can be spotty. Two good, deep-soaking storm episodes, correctly spaced, could ensure a harvest of these quick-maturing crops.

Some farmers still make use of *akĭ chiñ* agriculture. Their fields can be seen along the road from Nogales to Ímuris and Magdalena. In late summer and early fall, their milpas are lush and verdant. Although the farmers here today are probably mestizo, the technology they use was developed by the O'odham who formerly farmed these washes.

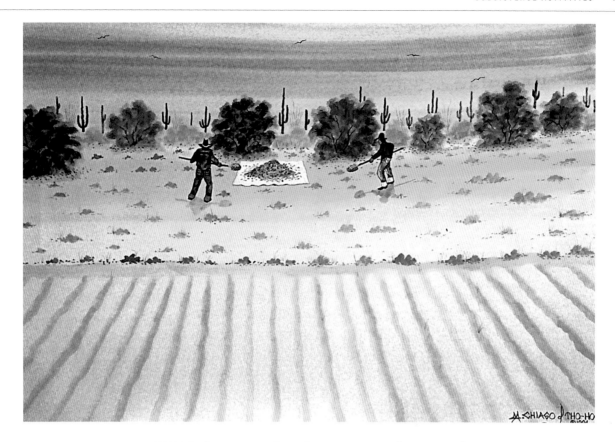

WHAT'S IN A WORD?: *WAKOLA (VAKOLA)*

These men at the edge of an *akĭ* are gathering *wakola* (*vakola*) to add to their fields.

When the sudden summer rains fill these desert washes, the water is filled with the nitrogen-rich dried leaflets of mesquite, ironwood, and paloverde that have accumulated during the long dry season. Mixed in are the abundant droppings of *totobĭ*, 'cottontails', and *chuuwĭ* (*chuuvĭ*), 'jackrabbits', that rest in the shade of tree-lined washes.

O'odham call this flotage *wakola* (*vakola*). Various authors have translated this as 'trash' or 'rubbish'. But to the O'odham, it is a precious gift of the storms, about which they sing songs and recite orations. In addition to what washes onto their fields with the first floodwaters, they may gather more to put on their fields, as shown here. It is their fertilizer.

Many O'odham words associated somehow with water have *va-* or *wa-* incorporated into them: *vatopĭ*, 'fish'; *vaamog*, 'mosquito'; *vakoañ*, 'heron, egret'; *vavukĭ*, 'Raccoon'; *vaapk*, 'reed'; *vaamul*, 'marshy area'; *vavhia*, 'well'; *vachki*, 'pond'. And, of course, *vakola*, the flood-borne fertilizer. Most Tohono O'odham dialects would pronounce these words *wa-*.

The Akimel O'odham irrigated directly from the larger desert streams. Some of their nutrients came from muddy river water, but they also left mesquite trees and other woody legumes standing in their fields and fence rows to enrich the soil. Even the River People practiced some *akĭ chiñ* agriculture into the early 1900s, an additional option in a harsh environment.

3

EVERYDAY LIFE

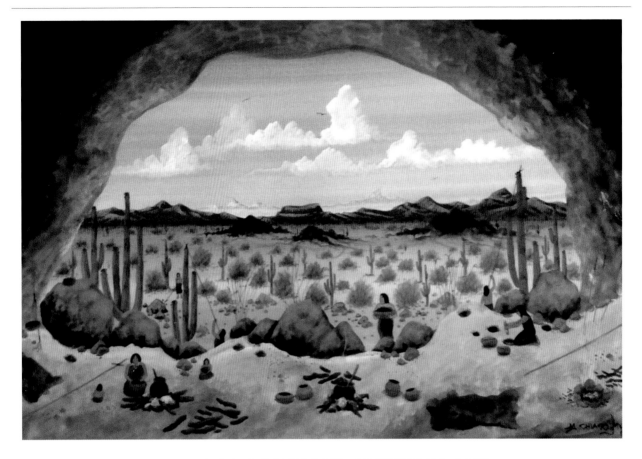

PREHISTORIC DAILY LIFE AT VENTANA CAVE

Ventana Cave in the northwestern part of the Tohono O'odham homelands is known in O'odham as Chio Wawhia (Chio Vavhia), 'cave well'. (There is a small spring at the back of the cave.) It is an opening facing east in the Castle Mountains, about 450 feet above the surrounding desert. The cave was excavated by the Arizona State Museum under the direction of Emil Haury and Julian Hayden in the early 1940s, yielding a ten-thousand-year record of human occupation and remains of many Pleistocene mammals now extinct.

Michael has chosen to paint daily activities from within the cave looking out toward the desert. Baboquivari Peak, prominent landmark in the Tohono O'odham homelands, can be seen on the distant horizon, 60 miles away. This is the only painting in the series depicting pre–European contact life of the O'odham.

Many daily activities familiar to more modern times are shown in this prehistoric scene. Women are picking Saguaro fruit and pounding mesquite pods in a bedrock mortar. Others are cooking *haashañ sitol* in ceramic ollas. Firewood and two animal hides for beds are scattered about. Pictographs are shown on the rock wall of the cave.

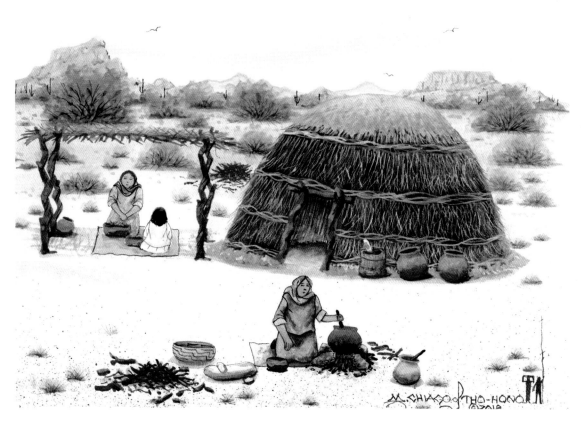

HISTORIC O'ODHAM *OLAS KII* OR ROUND HOUSE

The historic O'odham dwelling was an *olas kii*, 'round house', *o'olas kiikĭ* in the plural. Its internal structure was essentially the same as a *watto* (*vatto*): four sturdy forked upright posts or *horcones* in Spanish, called *cheechttondag*, with crossbeams or *vaupanadag*, 'vigas', stretched across them and smaller poles laid across the crossbeams. Then over this basic framework the *kikkio*, 'wall supports', made of *melhog*, 'Ocotillo branches', were inserted into the ground in a circle and their upper ends bent over and tied to make a half dome. Several horizontal roundhouse hoops or stays of Ocotillo, the *bishpadag*, circled the walls on the outside and were tied securely to the upright Ocotillo branches inside. This was then covered with *u'us kokomagĭ*, 'Arrowweed'; *oagam*, 'Seep-willow'; *huuñ va'ug*, 'cornstalks'; *vashai*, 'grass'; or some other light vegetation to form the walls. Finally, the whole structure might be covered with dirt or mud, usually around the base of the walls and on the top. There were no windows or smoke hole, and only a single low entryway facing east.

The Tohono O'odham *olas kii* tended to have a somewhat rounded roof, as the one Michael painted, but Akimel O'odham made a larger, broader *kii* with a more flattened roof, the shape of an overturned washbasin. For the internal supporting structure, they had access to larger trees along the river: *auppa*, 'cottonwood'; *che'ul*, 'willow'; *kui*, 'mature mesquite'. Various spectators could watch village events from the roof of the Akimel O'odham *kii*.

The *olas kii* was used for sleeping in rainy or cold weather and for storing belongings. A small fire might be built near the entrance for warming the small space. People slept on a woven mat called a *maiñ* that was rolled up and leaned against the wall during the daytime. But most activities took place outside. The *watto* (*vatto*) was the center of activity, providing protection from the burning sun while allowing cool breezes to pass through. For Akimel O'odham, an *uuksha*, a circle of upright Arrowweed, provided an open-air kitchen, protecting the fire and food from wind and blowing sand.

The house was torn down and burned at the death of the owner; however, the heavy beams—the *cheechttonḍag* and the *vavpanaḍag*—were too precious to be destroyed. Akimel O'odham salvaged them for a new house or placed them on the owner's pit grave holding down a covering of Arrowweed.

Around the beginning of twentieth century, *o'olas kiikĭ* were abandoned in favor of the rectangular *shaamt kii*: for Tohono O'odham, usually an adobe brick structure, for Akimel O'odham, a sandwich house of puddled adobe.

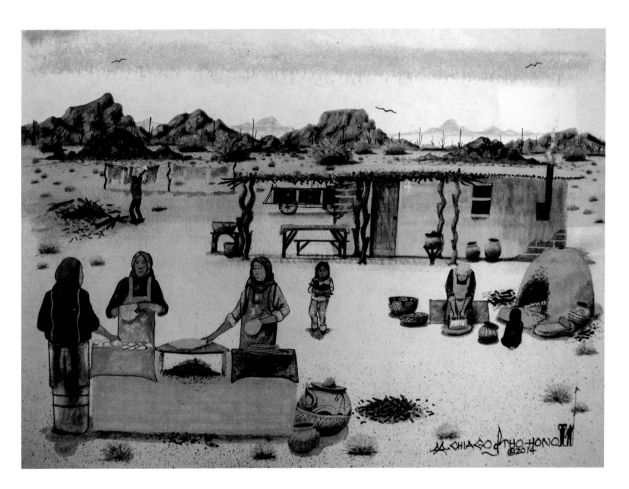

MODERN EVERYDAY LIFE

Daily life in an O'odham family included many activities, some shown in this painting.

The family compound is usually made up of at least one *kii*, or sometimes several *kiikĭ*, with a *watto* (*vatto*) nearby. In the desert, many daily activities took place under the *vatto*. It is roofed with *melhog* or leafy rods of *u'us kokomagĭ* or some other brush.

Here at one end of the *vatto* is a basin and bucket of precious water for washing clothes, now hanging on the clothesline. At the other end is a *va'igkuḍ*, an olla made of semiporous clay for cooling *va'igĭ*, 'drinking water'. It sits on a three-branched mesquite post called a *ha'adaikuḍ*. Also under the *vatto* is the dining table covered with red oilcloth. Here the family eats, weather permitting.

Near the door, each house is marked with a willow branch or Creosote Bush cross that is blessed on Día de la Santa Cruz (May 3), a tradition inherited from the Yaquis and Mayos and other Sonoran Catholics.

The women are engaged in the daily activity of making *pilkan chechemait*, 'wheat tortillas'. Prior to European contact, *huuñ*, 'corn or maize', would have been used, but after contact, the O'odham adopted wheat, a crop that would be raised in the cooler winter season. A woman kneels near the *ol-nĭio* or *paantakuḍ*, 'outdoor oven', grinding wheat on a *machchuḍ* or *chu'ikuḍ*, 'grindstone', with a *viidakuḍ*, 'mano'. The resulting flour is *chu'i*. At the end of the grindstone, the flour falls into a *vaagakuḍ* or *vachiho*, 'wooden mixing bowl'.

At the *naadakuḍ* (also *istŭvho*, *istúúkva*), 'adobe stove', one woman pats the moistened flour into dough balls. Another slaps and stretches a ball into a thin tortilla that eventually will reach to the crook of her arm, while a third flips the finished *chemait* over a hot *komal* to toast on one side, then on the other. Mesquite wood, which burns with a hot, even flame, provides the coals to heat the *komal*. This may be a disc blade or the removed end of a fifty-gallon metal barrel. In the days of corn tortillas, this would have been a smaller clay *komal*.

The domed *ol-nĭio* (from Spanish *hornillo*) is characteristic of the Pueblo villages of the Southwest but is also found among the Tohono O'odham. Its ultimate roots are neither Spanish nor Native American but Arabic North African by way of the Moors of southern Spain. Hispanic colonizers introduced it to the New World. Here it is used to bake small loaves or tortas of wheat bread usually to be served on feast days.

To the back, a man chops mesquite limbs from a large pile of wood delivered by wagon. Mesquite grows mostly in the foothills and along the banks of an *akĭ*. A boy keeps the women supplied with fuel. *Chechemait*-making is hot work. Next to the stove is a decorated *va'igkuḍ* of water with a *ha'u*, 'gourd dipper', tied to the top.

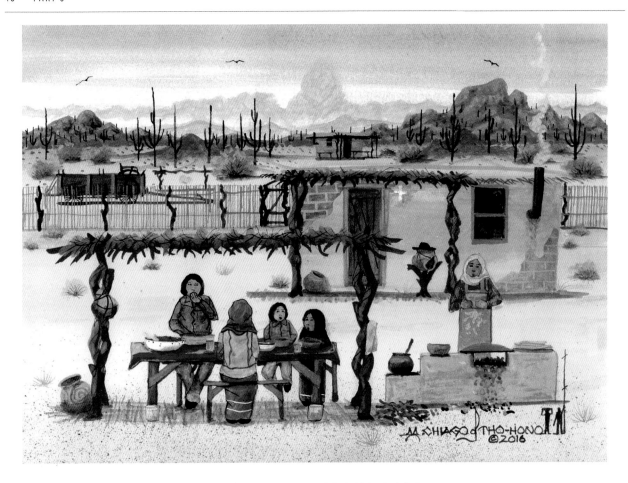

DAILY LIFE IN THE VILLAGE

Here a family is having lunch or dinner under the shade of the *vatto*. The outdoor table is covered with a red oilcloth. The bowls might be filled with *chuukug hidoḍ*, a red chile stew with hunks of beef cooked until they begin to fall apart. *O'olas ko'okol*, tiny, fiery red chiles known in English as chiltepins, and *on*, 'salt', are favorite seasonings. If this is spring, bowls of boiled red *kuavul*, 'wolfberry or squawberry', might be served. The bushes produce their small orange-red fruits even after dry winters.

For beans to taste right, they must be cooked in a clay *ha'a*, shown to the cook's right. These thick-walled blackened pots are prized possessions, particularly today when few O'odham women make ceramics. The beans may be *muuñ*, 'common bean', either pinto or pink beans, though these seem to be more recent additions to the O'odham diet. The traditional bean is *bawĭ* (*bavĭ*), 'tepary', a very small bean domesticated from wild ancestors in the desert and mountains. *Toota bavĭ*, 'white tepary', and *oam bavĭ*, 'brown tepary', appear at village feast days and can be found in reservation stores. The tepary is excellently adapted to dry farming in the desert and out-produces other species of beans.

The fence behind the house is made of *melhog* planted in the ground and strung together with barbed wire between mesquite posts. Often the *melhog* take root and form a living fence that lasts, leafing out whenever rains come.

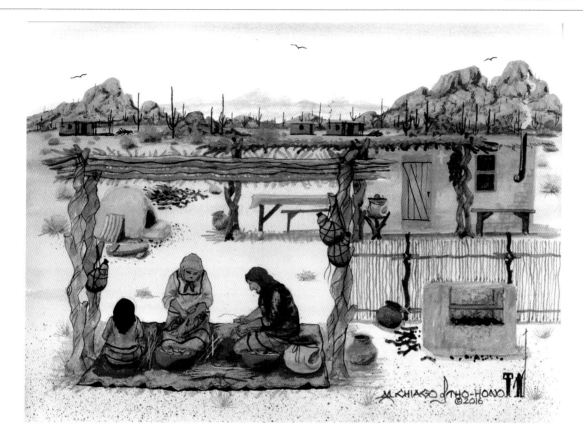

BASKET WEAVING

The O'odham were renowned for their *hohoa* or *huhua*, 'coiled baskets', some woven so tightly they were water-tight (see painting on page 81 of wine serving). These women work in the shade of the *watto* (*vatto*), though at an earlier time, most of the weaving took place in the *huhulga kii*, 'menstrual hut', a ways from the village. This earth-covered hut kept the weaving materials from drying out too fast in the desert air, while secluding the women during their menses.

Bundles of fibers lie on the blanket while others soak in clay bowls. The woman on the left is punching a hole through a coil with her *owij* (*ovij*), 'awl', while the woman on the right has already put a strand through and is pulling it tight. The little girl is learning. She will make a small basket—her first—and present it to some mentor, an older woman who is a good basket weaver. This will ensure that she inherits the elder's skills. A large tray basket may take a weaver more than a year to complete.

The *naadakuḍ* to the right is more often found in O'odham yards and feast grounds than the Pueblo-style oven shown behind the weavers. It is an adobe structure with a horizontal grill and lacks a chimney. Large pots can be set atop the wall. A fire of *kui ku'agĭ*, 'mesquite wood', is built on the open shelf below the grate. The darkened *ha'a* to the left of the stove is for cooking beans such as *muuñ* or *bawĭ* (*bavĭ*). A metate and mano sit next to the outdoor oven at the left.

Two ristras of dry stringed chiles, usually bought on the annual fall pilgrimage to Magdalena, hang from the *watto*. These are used throughout the year to make chile stew.

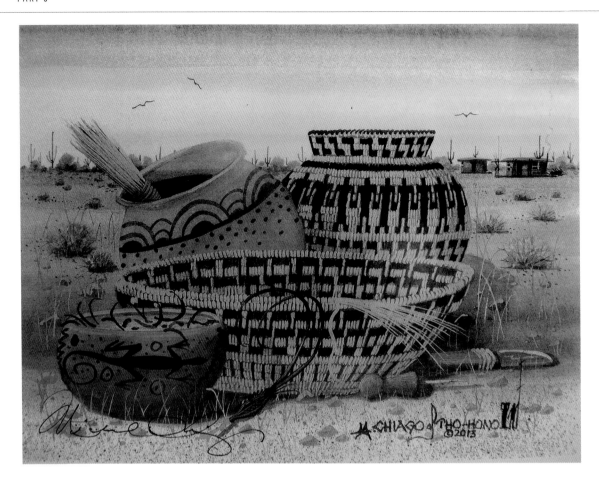

BASKETRY MATERIALS

O'odham women made both bowl baskets (shown here) and the flatter tray baskets that found many uses in everyday activities. Both types used the coiled basketry technique.

The foundation of the coiled baskets varied according to availability of material. For Akimel O'odham, it was the split flower stalk of the *uḍuwhag* (*uḍvak*), 'cattail', while for Tohono O'odham, it was usually *moho*, 'Bear-grass'. Over this foundation is sewn young shoots of *che'ul*, 'willow', peeled and split in half. This makes the white part of the design, usually the background. The black comes from the seed pod of *ihug*, 'devil's claw' (*Proboscidea*, Martyniaceae). In Michael's painting, a pod is shown in front of the basket while leathery strips peeled from the "horns" soak in a dish. Some grew *ihug* in their gardens to maintain a variety most suitable for weaving; those with long "claws" that were easily peeled and pliant were most sought after. The weaver also wanted strips that were uniformly black, not gray.

Tohono O'odham weavers today use mostly *takui*, 'Soaptree Yucca or Palmilla', for coiling. The tender central leaves are broken off the plant; the greener outer leaves retain their color, while the inner ones are sun-bleached white. A bundle of *takui* ready for weaving is in the back *ha'a*. Yucca leaves are more easily and quickly manipulated than the willow splints, though less durable. Willow and devil's claw baskets, when they can be found, command a much higher price than yucca baskets.

The weaver's tools lie at the front. The *owij* (*ovij*) has a distinctive shape so it can be kept between the weaver's ring and middle fingers as she pushes a splint through the opening she has just made using her other fingers. The small knife is to trim the coil materials to the width and thickness she wants; she also will trim the butt end of a splint when the strip ends or she changes color.

In historic times, certain villages of Tohono O'odham would come north to the Gila River to help with the annual wheat harvest. This was a time for exchange of goods. Tohono O'odham weavers sought the long-clawed *ihug* that the Akimel O'odham raised, as well as the young willow shoots that once grew abundantly along the river and creeks. Some gathered cattail flower stalks for basket foundations. Men traded for blanks of *u'us kokomagĭ* that grew along streams and the Akimel O'odham irrigation ditches. These cut and shaved blanks were called *sheesha* or *sheeshelna* (singular *shelna*).

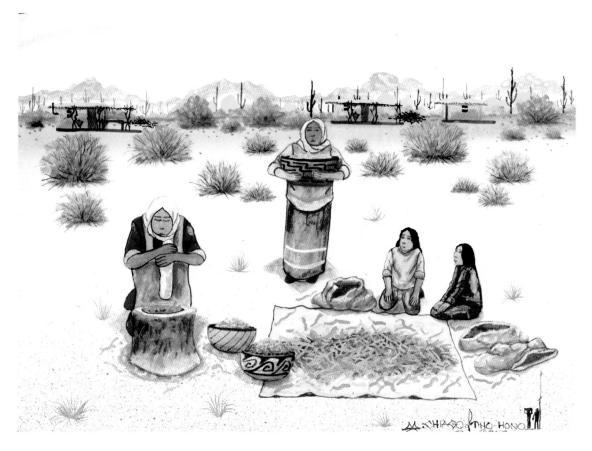

O'ODHAM WOMEN PREPARING MESQUITE PODS

The driest pods could be processed in mesquite camp; the rest were taken home and stored in a large Arrow-weed granary called a *homta* for use throughout the year. These *hohomta* baskets once festooned the tops of every Akimel O'odham house and *vatto*. Additional ones were in yards, fenced off from horses and cattle that also relished the *vihog*.

The hygroscopic pods were spread out on the hot ground to dry, as shown in this painting. Note that the women are not working under a shady *vatto* but out in the full, hot sun. Using a *cheepidakuḍ*, 'stone pestle', one woman pounds the *vihog* in a *chepa*, a wooden mortar made of a mesquite or cottonwood log. The resulting mash could be mixed with water and strained or boiled to make a very rich, sweet drink called *wa'u* (*va'u*). Or the mash could be sifted in a special basket, a *gigidakuḍ*, to make a flour called *vihog chu'i*. This in turn was stored in a special basket called a *vashom*, or made into *wa'u* (*va'u*), a hard loaf called *cheeg* or *komkĭchuḍ*, or a pudding called *kui hidoḍ*. There were also other ways of preparing the *vihog*. Akimel O'odham said that something made from mesquite appeared at just about every meal.

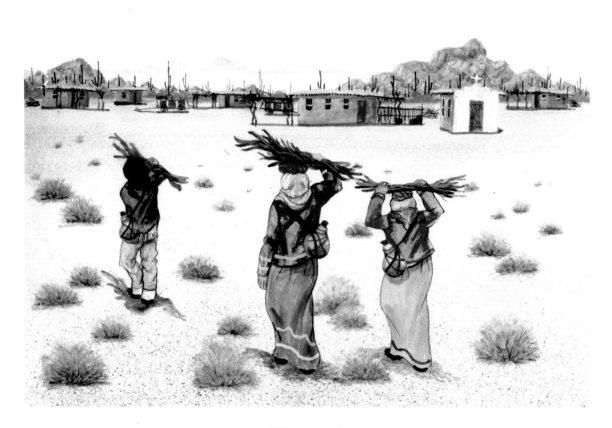

FIREWOOD

Fuel for cooking fires and for heating the small adobe homes as well as outdoor fires for festive events had to be gathered in the desert, particularly along rivers and arroyos.

The fine-grained wood of *kui* was, and for some still is, the firewood of choice. *Ho'idkam*, 'Desert Ironwood', might be used, but it is so dense that it resists cutting and produces such a hot fire that it might burn out a metal stove. While common, the two paloverde species, *kuk chehedagĭ* and *ko'okmaḍkĭ*, have much softer woods but still are not preferred because they are said to produce disagreeable odors or even harmful smoke.

Many smaller shrubs were used for *taimuñig*, 'kindling', also called *haupal kosh*, 'Red-tailed Hawk's nest'. These three women have been gathering this lighter wood.

Big piles of *ku'agĭ*, 'firewood', are usually found outside O'odham dwellings, as shown here and in many of Michael's other paintings. Generally, men are responsible for bringing wagonloads of wood into the village, while women—even elderly ones—are often seen at the woodpile, swinging an axe and chopping the day's supply.

Mesquite makes a good bed of coals, which are used not only for cooking but also for making *haakĭ chu'i*, 'pinole or parched wheat flour'. On cold winter nights, some families burned a washtub of mesquite wood outside, then dragged the tub of coals inside to warm the house all night.

During feast day dances in winter and nighttime ceremonies, a man would take shovels full of coals from the big fire and spread them around under the benches to warm the feet and legs of seated spectators.

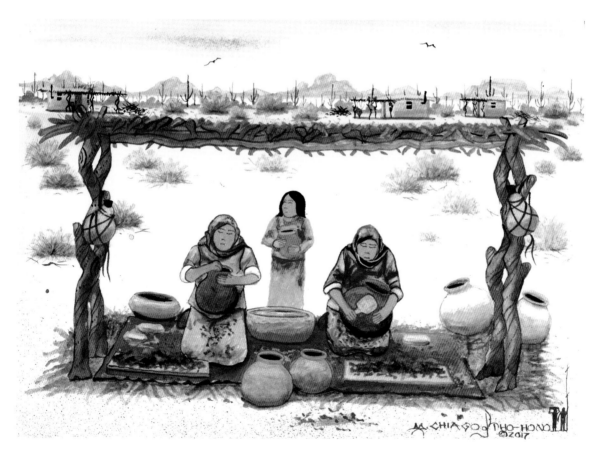

POTTERY MAKING

Once almost all utilitarian wares were made by O'odham ceramicists. A few women still make water ollas and bean pots.

Bid, 'clay', is mined from traditional pits, crushed, and sifted. When ready for use, the clay is moistened, kneaded, rolled into coils, and built up a few rolls at a time. These are then pounded into shape with a wooden paddle. This is repeated until the vessel reaches the intended size. When finished, the pot is set aside in the shade to dry. Finally, it is fired in a shallow open pit using a soft wood or cow pies.

A large *ha'a* intended for a water container is made with special clay. The finished product must be porous, allowing water to seep through the walls, cooling the water inside by evaporation. These sit on a three-branched mesquite olla stand called a *ha'a-daikuḍ*. These can be seen in the shade of the *vatto* at two of the houses in the background.

A pot made for cooking, on the other hand, should be impermeable. It may be further sealed with tallow, making it still less permeable.

A slip of *wegĭ* (*vegĭ*) *bid*, 'red clay', or *hedt*, 'ochre or iron oxide', is sometimes used to give the vessel a brighter red color. If a pot is to be decorated, it is painted with a liquid made by boiling *kui ushab*, 'mesquite sap', then the pot is refired. This gives a black design. Most utility ware was left undecorated.

Although *haha'a*, 'clay vessels', were used for cooking pots, bowls, water coolers, and for fermenting *haashañ navait*, they are fragile. For water canteens in the desert, where a clay container might easily drop and break, the *wakoa* (*vakoa, vako*), 'bottle gourd', was prized. And a gourd was much lighter than a ceramic vessel. These women have hung their *wapkoa* from the posts of the *watto* where they are working. Traditionally women carried water in clay ollas on their heads while men used the bottle gourd canteen.

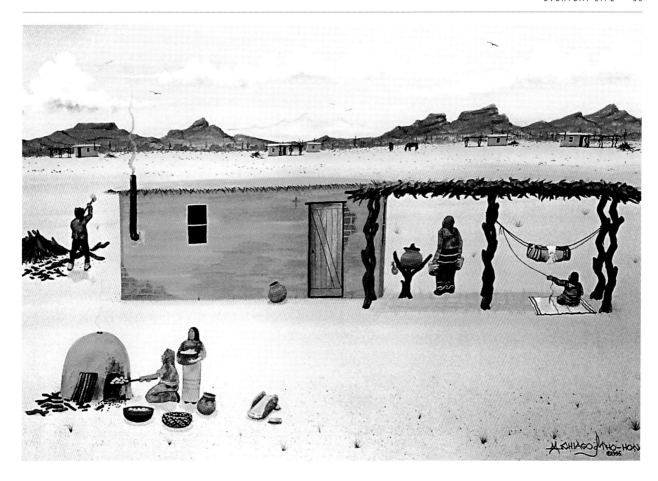

VILLAGE ACTIVITIES AND DAILY LIFE: BABY SWING

In the hot country, much of daily life occurred outside under the *watto* (*vatto*). Here sat the *va'igkuḍ*, 'clay water cooler', and women worked on their baskets or ceramics, as in the paintings on pages 49 and 53.

Babies had their own swing or hammock called a *viḍutakuḍ* or *ulukuḍ* (from the verbs 'to swing' or 'to rock'). This was made of two ropes tied to the support poles of the *vatto* with a soft blanket cross-folded between them, making a safe receptacle for the baby. A small pillow supported the infant's head with a smaller cloth wrapped around the swing making the entire arrangement secure. Finally, a woman could rock the cradle hammock by pulling gently on a rope attached to the cross-ropes while she worked nearby. This arrangement may still be seen.

At an earlier time, a mother put her baby in an elaborate portable cradleboard called an *ali wulkuḍ*, somewhat similar to those of other North American Indians. A mesquite root was bent into a U shape, then thin flat *waapai* (*vaapai*) were latched on as crosspieces. The projecting curve served as a handle. A basketry hoodpiece finished the cradleboard. The fine inner bark of the cottonwood or willow tree covered with a cotton cloth provided the mattress. Once the baby was comfortably asleep, it was taken out.

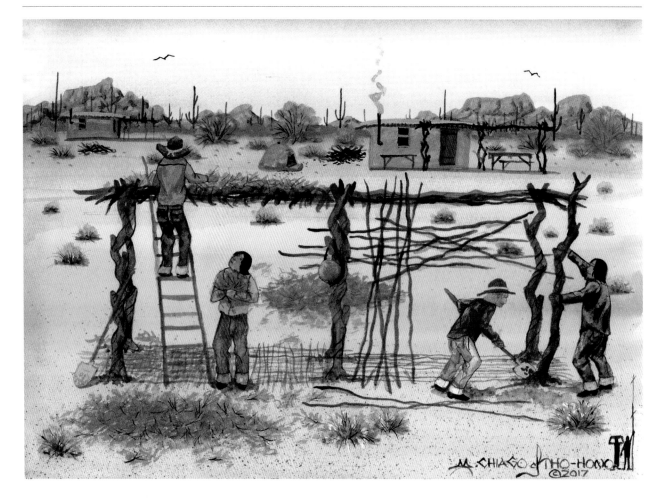

CONSTRUCTING THE *WATTO* (*VATTO*)

Just about every O'odham household had a *vatto*, either freestanding or attached to the house itself. Sometimes it was in a breezeway joining two adjacent adobe buildings. The *vatto* had no walls, allowing free passage of desert breezes while providing shade from the relentless sun of much of the year.

The structure was usually made of four, six, or nine upright mesquite or cottonwood posts called *chechtton-ḍag*. These uprights or *horcones* were forked on top to receive the horizontal vigas or *vavanaḍag*, 'stretchers' or 'cross-beams', also of mesquite. Laid across these were the *latillas* or long branches of *melhog* or *kui*, or the light and thin *waapai* (*vaapai*). The final covering, providing the actual shade, varied according to locality. River People used the long, leafy stems of *u'us kokomagĭ* that grew to 8 feet or taller along the desert streams and ditches. Desert People, shown in this painting, used the sticky branches of *shegoi* (*shegi*). In modern times, chicken wire might be spread across the top to keep the leafy branches in place. Otherwise, *siswulokĭ* (*sisivulokĭ*), 'remolindos or whirlwinds', might blow the cover away.

4
—

SOCIAL LIFE

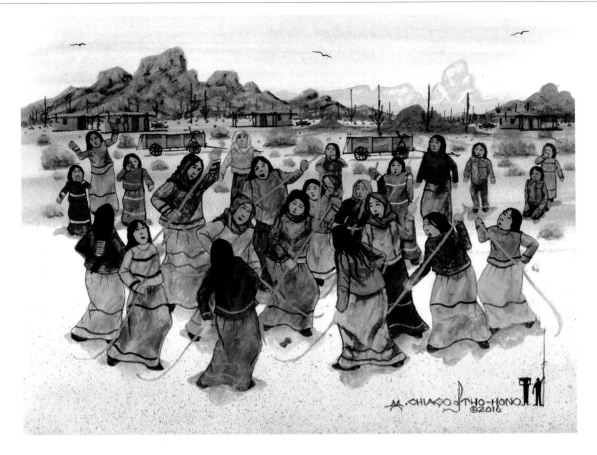

TOKAḌA PLAYERS

Both Tohono and Akimel O'odham women and girls play a game of double-ball shinny called *tokaḍa* (*toka*, *tokal*).

Goals were set up 200 to 400 yards apart and the field cleared for playing. Two women, good *tokaḍa* players, chose other women to make up the two teams. Any number was acceptable as long as the teams were equal. Each player had an *usaga*, a stick 4 feet or longer, curved at the bottom and slightly pointed. The ball or puck, called an *ola*, was a section of rope, bark, or braided leather with a knot or wooden ball at each end.

At the middle of the field, a game leader tossed the double-ball up and players scrambled to hook and fling it in the direction of their goal. Normally mild-mannered girls and older women suddenly became aggressive players. Dust flew, sticks clashed, and pity the dog that was unwise enough to get into the melee. Any player who touched the ball with her hands was eliminated from her team. The game was over when one team succeeded finally in getting the ball over their goal line.

There were specific *toka* songs sung on the eve of the game, which was once accompanied by heavy betting. Mythology recounts the story of a young woman who was so inordinately fond of intervillage *tokal* games that she neglected her nursing child who sank into the sand of an arroyo and became the first Saguaro cactus. When his mother deprives him of life-giving liquid, he becomes the source of the juicy Saguaro fruit, which is made into a cooling drink and the *navait* for the wine feast, which in turn calls down the summer monsoons.

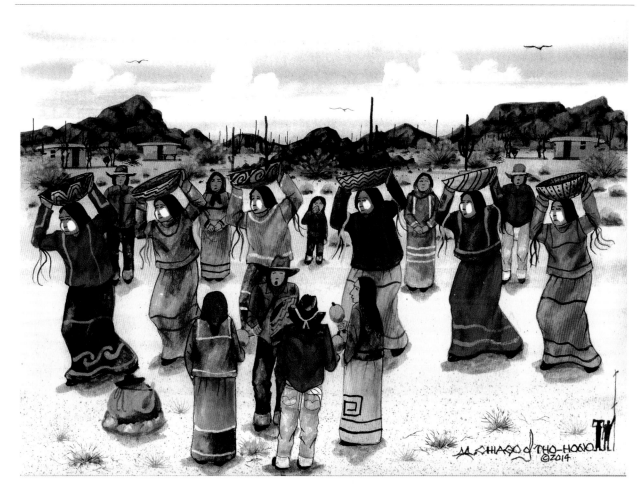

HUA KEIHINA (HUA CHUUDKĬ), 'BASKET DANCE'

Unlike most dances, the *hua keihina* (*hua chuudkĭ*), 'basket dance', had no ceremonial significance. It might be called *hoakaj* (*huakaj*) *keihina* or *hoakaj* (*huakaj*) *chuudkĭ*. Originally it was a formal opportunity for maidens to show off their homemaking skills by displaying baskets they had woven. Young men among the spectators would vie for the girl they wished to court. It was a social occasion for adolescents to become acquainted.

One of the singers keeps time with an overturned basket, the O'odham equivalent of a drum. The bottom of the basket drum, its *atchuda*, is made of black devil's claw, which is more durable than willow. The songs were often about the desert and the creatures that live there. One humorous song compares a bowlegged cowboy to a *kuaḍagĭ*, a species of ant with long, thin legs.

When an O'odham girl came of age, a celebration called Wuagida, a puberty ceremony, was held in her honor. Several girls might celebrate at the same time. If the family had enough resources, the Wuagida dancing might continue for several nights. Subsequently, the basket dance provided an opportunity for eligible girls to be the focus of the community's attention. In modern times, the dance has lost this meaning, with older women participating.

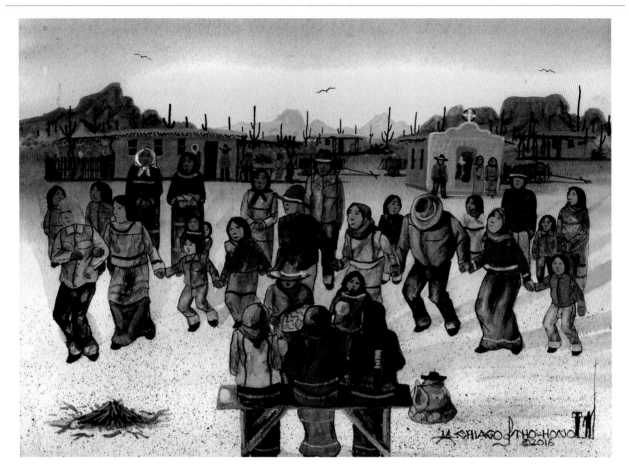

KEIHINA (*CHUUDKĬ*), 'CIRCLING DANCE'

As night falls on the village on feast day, singers who know the *keihina* (also known as *chuudkĭ* or *sikol himda*), 'circling dance', songs gather in a cleared space and begin singing. The right hand of each singer holds a *shawikuḍ* (*shavikuḍ*), 'gourd rattle'. One keeps time by beating on the bottom of tray basket or today usually an overturned cardboard box. The lead singer begins with a powerful voice, and the other males follow. Women join in harmony with the men.

Soon dancers begin to assemble in couples, joining hands and arms with the lead dancer. As in ceremonies, the dancers move in a counterclockwise direction: one step to the right, then the left foot is brought up against it with a vertical bounce of the body. As other couples join the line, a circle is formed around the chorus, closing the line. If still more dancers join, a second line around the first may form.

A single song has four to six lines, but there are repetitions of a specific order. When the song is completed, it is sung through all the sets of repetitions three more times. Certain songs require the dancers to reverse the direction to clockwise before resuming the usual the movement to the right. The signal is given by the lead singer or dancer, here shown as an older man.

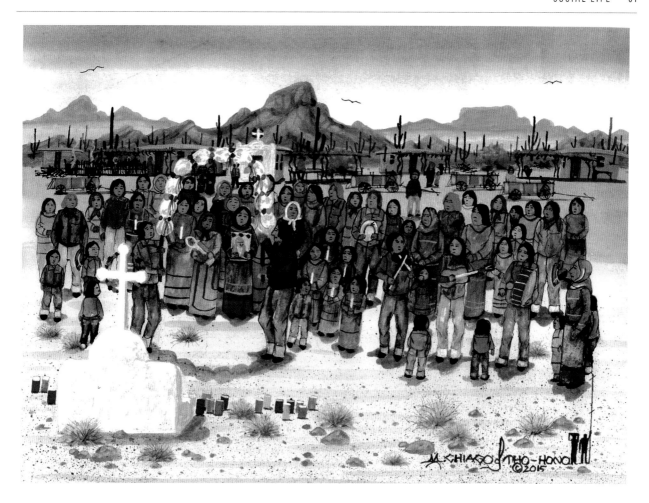

VILLAGE FEAST DAY CELEBRATION

Each major village has a church dedicated to a patron saint. The saint's day in the liturgical calendar is one occasion for a village celebration. The feast may combine elements of conventional Catholicism and the *saanto himdag,* a local blend of Mexican Catholicism and traditional practices.

The occasion calls for considerable preparation. The village grounds are swept clean. The church, feast house, cooking area, and dance area must be refurbished and decorated with crepe-paper flowers made for the occasion. One or more beeves are killed and butchered. This all takes days.

In this painting, the people have processed out of the small church with the white façade. Leading the way are people carrying sacred images from both the church altar and their homes—here a statue and a holy picture. Others shower confetti on the marching, singing people.

The community walks toward a *koḍs,* a monument cross about 300 feet east of the church door. Multicolored votive candles burn around the processional monument. Two men bear a *kiohoḍ,* a processional arch decorated with ribbons and paper flowers, ahead of the sacred images. Such arches are of ancient origin and were noted in the diaries of Father Eusebio Kino and other early Jesuits to make contact with the O'odham. Musicians accompany the group, playing violin, guitar, and drum. They sing a traditional song in Spanish.

At the *koḍs*, villagers may say the rosary, then return slowly to the church and process around it before the statues and holy pictures are replaced on the altar. Mass follows when a priest, usually a Franciscan friar, is available.

Meanwhile, back in the cooking area to the left, some women have been preparing food for the feast: *muuñ hidoḍ*, 'pinto beans'; *chuukug hidoḍ* or *ko'okol hidoḍ*, 'hot beef and red chile stew'; *paan*, 'oven-baked wheat buns'; and of course plenty of *chechemait*, 'wheat tortillas'. In Akimel O'odham country, traditional foods such as *baviˇ* and *hannam* may round out the menu. A pile of mesquite wood lies outside the cooking stockade, and smoke rises from the cook stove and oven.

The feast house just next to the cooking enclosure is furnished with long tables and wooden benches. When prayers are finished in the church, the community retires here to eat. Many visitors have arrived from other villages and even off-reservation, as Michael has shown with the wagons parked on each side of the church. All will be fed in turn. All are guests of the village.

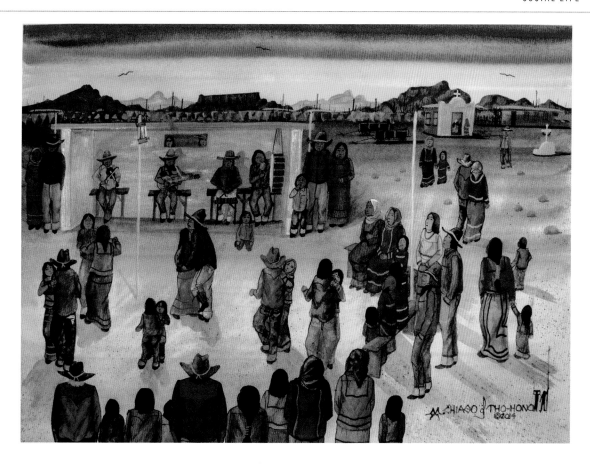

WAILA, 'SOCIAL DANCING'

In addition to the *sikol himda*, with its cycles of traditional O'odham songs—really sung poetry—there is a Western-style social dance, or *waila*, at village feast days. The name *waila* comes from the Spanish word *baile*. Akimel O'odham often call this chicken scratch. In any case, it is thoroughly borderlands Mexican American in style.

As with the church and feast house, the dance ground is cleaned and decorated with paper flowers and flags. The musicians sit in a *mumsigo ha kii* (*wailakuḍ kii*), 'enclosure or bandstand', facing the plaza or dance area. The violin is played as a fiddle. In this painting, a guitar and drum complete the suite of instruments. With the advent of electricity in more recent times, the band will include acoustic guitar, electric base, accordion, saxophone, and a drum set—and considerably more volume.

There is no age segregation. Everyone from youngsters scarcely able to walk to the elderly who will worry about their arthritic joints the next day take advantage of the lively music. At an earlier time, men danced only with men and women with women, but that stricture has long since dissolved. Couples dance with great precision, as if a single entity. They circle the dance floor counterclockwise, as with all O'odham movements.

The music is a Mexican version of Old World polka, *waila*, and *choodi*, a simpler two-step. A very popular *cumbia* will get everyone from the oldest to the youngest out to circle the *wailakuḍ*, 'dance floor'. In Tohono O'odham country, Western-style dancing may continue throughout the night until the sun comes up.

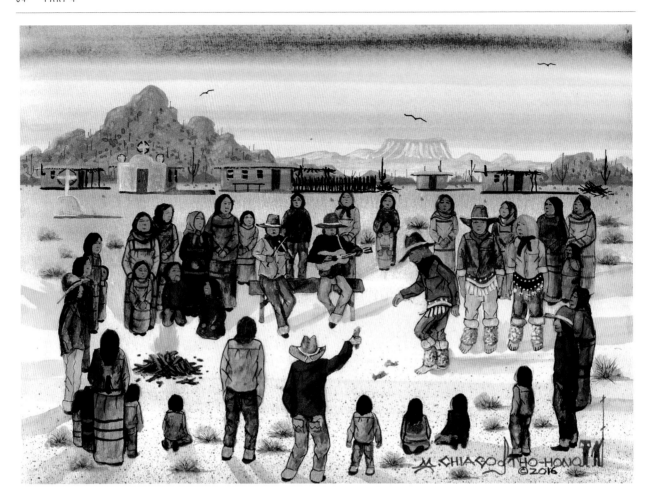

PAPKO'OLA DANCERS

The Pako'ola Dancer adds to the entertainment of many village events, including the village saint's day feast, as Michael has shown in this painting. The O'odham name is taken from the Pascola (*Pahko'ola*) Dancers of the Yaqui and Mayo of Sonora, the probable prototype. Pascola takes its name from Easter or Pascua.

At one time both Akimel O'odham and the various Tohono O'odham groups had Pascola Dancers. Their purpose is to amuse and, unlike the solemn Deer Dancers, they may engage in humorous banter directly with the village spectators. Often they perform at night.

Three Papko'ola Dancers are shown at the right. Two have broad leather belts with shell rattles, and the third has metal sleigh bells dangling from his belt. Strings of *kokswul* (*koksvul*), 'cocoons', filled with sand are wrapped around their lower legs. They are barefoot and perform intricate steps, showing off individual dexterity. Unlike the Yaqui and Mayo Pascola dancers, the O'odham shown here wear shirts and have no masks.

Two Papko'ola musicians sit on a bench, one with a guitar, the other a violin played fiddle style. While they play a repetitive tune, spectators will throw crumpled bills into the dance area and the Pako'ola Dancer will attempt to pick them up with his mouth while dancing.

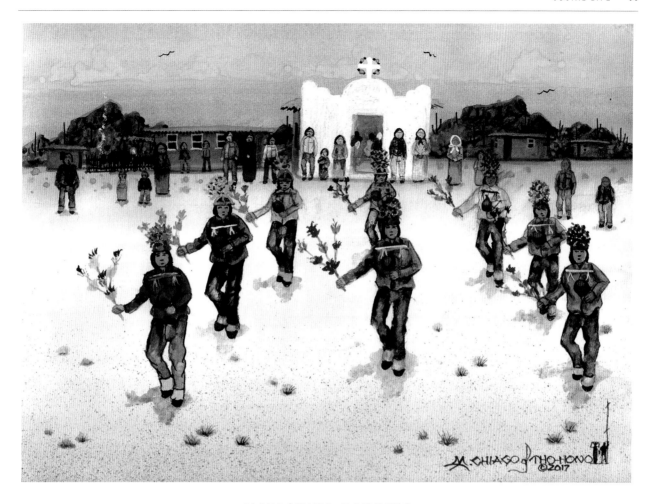

MATACHINA DANCERS

On special occasions such as church feast days, a group of sacred dancers may perform before, during, or after Mass. These boys and men belong to an organization dedicated to the Blessed Virgin. The origin of Matachina dancers is wholly European, though its introduction probably predates the Jesuit expulsion of 1767, at least among the Yaqui and Mayo.

Matachina dancers often wear brightly colored ribbon shirts. Each carries a three-pronged wand in his right hand, decorated with brightly dyed feathers, and a red-painted *shawikuḍ* (*shavikuḍ*) in his left. On his head is a tall crown decorated with more feathers and crepe paper. The music is supplied by stringed instruments and drum, usually today played on a tape recorder.

Dancers begin outside church near the ceremonial cross, kneeling on one knee and crossing themselves. Then the lines of dancers—often more than shown here—begin their intricate steps. They wave their wands and swing them as they make graceful turns, weaving in and out and maintaining their footwork. The people watch with joyful reverence because this is a communal prayer. The culmination of the ceremony is when they dance into the church and kneel before the front altar.

5

RELIGIOUS LIFE

Shrines

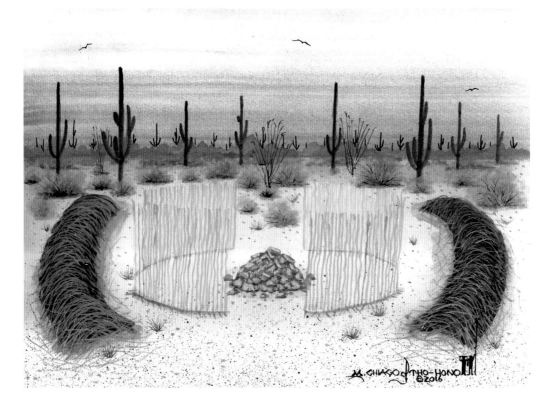

CHILDREN'S SHRINE

There are *hiaha'iñ* (*hiha'iñ*), 'sacred places or shrines' scattered throughout Pimería Alta. One of the best known to the O'odham, Children's Shrine, is near Kaij Mek (Santa Rosa).

The origin of Children's Shrine is found in legend. A man was out hunting and chased an animal, some say a *kaawĭ* (*kaav*), 'badger', a tabooed creature, down a hole. When he tried to retrieve the animal, winds or floodwaters came rushing out of the hole, threatening destruction of the earth. No offerings were effective. An older man said that four children—two boys and two girls—should be put down the opening as a sacrifice. Some say each came from a different clan. When this was done, the hole closed and a flood was averted.

The shrine itself, which covers the hole, is a pile of flat rocks (20 by 30 feet). It is enclosed in a palisade of peeled Ocotillo branches with openings in the four directions. Every two years, with special songs and ceremonies, the poles are pulled out and replaced with new ones, the old ones piled at two sides. The work is under the direction of the four nearest villages: Aangam, Akĭ Chiñ, Ge Aji, and Kaij Mek. Should the renewal ritual not be observed, a flood or wind would again emerge to destroy the earth. Offerings such as beads, shells, coins, or colored glass are made to the four flood children, who are considered to be still alive below.

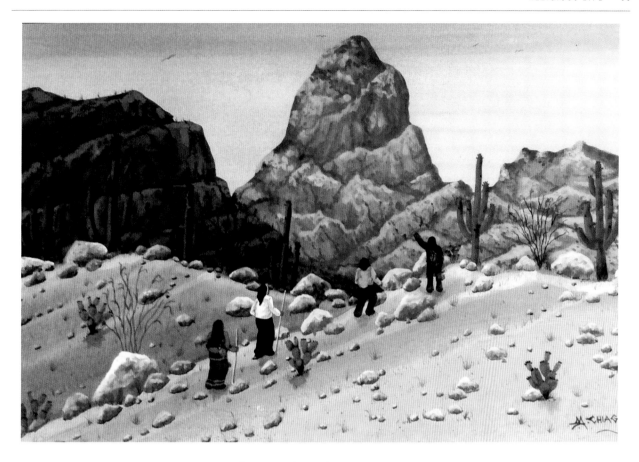

PILGRIMAGE TO I'ITOI'S *KII*

O'odham country is generously sprinkled with *hiahiñ* (*hiaha'iñ*, *hiha'iñ*) and other sacred places. Some of these are associated with one of the four original culture heroes, I'itoi or Se'ehe, also known as Elder Brother. Tohono O'odham more frequently call him I'itoi and look to him for help in times of difficulty.

At least three of his residences are still remembered. (There should be four, but apparently no one recalls the fourth one.) One of I'itoi's *kiikĭ* is in the southern tip of the South Mountains near Laveen. Another is somewhere in the volcanic caves of the Pinacate Peaks of Sonora. The third and most famous is at the west base of Waw Giwlik (Vav Giwulk), the uppermost peak in the Baboquivari Mountains along the eastern edge of the main Tohono O'odham reservation.

Here pilgrims are shown climbing up the trail to I'itoi's *kii*; one is a Franciscan sister. It's an arduous trek from the nearest road.

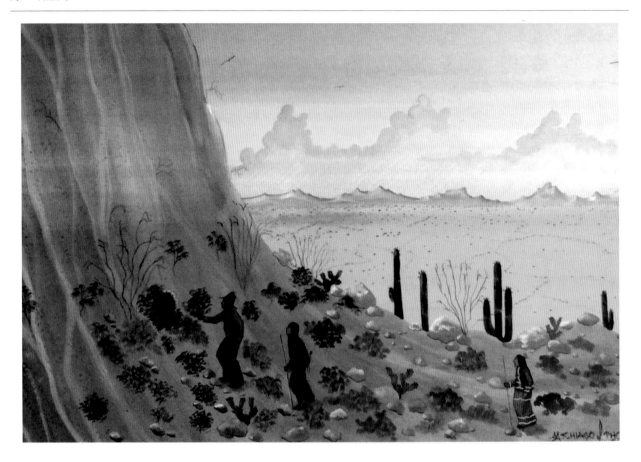

I'ITOI'S *KII*

There is only a small entrance to I'itoi's *kii*, usually covered with brush. At this cave, as at any other O'odham shrine, the pilgrim is expected to leave an offering, such as coins, beads, an arrow, a rifle cartridge, a shell, an oddly shaped stone, or some small personal item. Sometimes a twig of *shegoi*, an important medicinal plant, is left on a shrine.

A story is told locally that one of the Franciscan sisters visited I'itoi's cave in the Baboquivaris with some of her O'odham students. The youngsters each left an offering and went out. The nun thought she didn't need to leave anything and tried to exit, but the cave opening became too small. The boys shouted, "Sister, leave something!" She gave the only thing she had—her rosary—and the cave opened enough for her to get out.

Access to the area by nontribal members is only by special hiking permit issued at the district office in Ḍo Bawui (Topawa), Arizona.

Shamanism

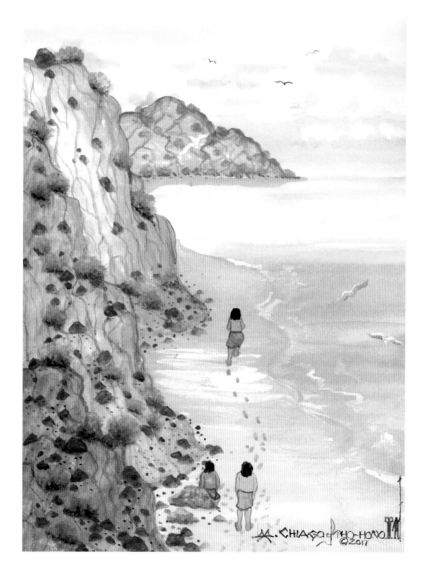

THE SOURCE OF SONGS (*ÑEÑE'I*, 'SUNG POETRY')

Materially the O'odham, like other members of the Northwest Mexican Ranchería complex, lived relatively simply. But the Desert People were exceedingly rich in an elaboration of *ñeñe'i*, 'sung poetry or songs'. Both men and women might have at their command hundreds of songs that could be recalled as occasion demanded.

A *ñe'i*, 'song', was a poem of four or more lines, repeated in a set pattern, then the whole set sung through four times. The language, called "song language," was modified to fit the rhythm of the verse, much like a Gregorian Kyrie, but not that simple. Songs might be about plants, animals, or something else in the desert environment such clouds, wind, lightning, or mountains. Songs were often in mirrored pairs with just the subject and the action differing: the Golden Eagle does something; the Prairie Falcon does something else. Sometimes they were in long sequences with an underlying theme—desert travel, for instance.

Songs were acquired by someone in a dream or trance after fasting and physical exertion. An animal might come to the person and teach him or her a song, giving that person power. That animal became one's personal helper. If someone was visited by a *ñuwĭ* (*ñui*), 'Turkey Vulture or buzzard', the person would be called a *ñui namkam*, 'buzzard meeter'.

Youth sought a dream helper because with the song also came power, perhaps in racing, gambling, locating the enemy when on the warpath, calling rain, or diagnosing or curing sickness. The helper taught the meeter his or her specialization or vocation. For instance, the *ñui namkam* would be called to sing songs at a *wusosig*, a healing for *ñui mumkidag*, 'buzzard sickness'.

There were more occasions for men to acquire power and songs, but women might be recipients as well. For young men, the salt pilgrimage to the Gulf of California was an opportunity to run for miles along the beach until overtaken with exhaustion. Then a white egret or gull or even the ocean in person might appear to him and give him power and songs. This is what Michael has shown in this painting.

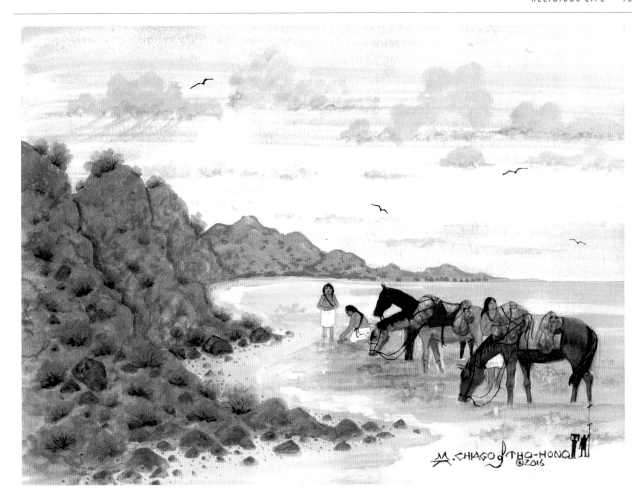

SALT PILGRIMAGE

The summer salt pilgrimage to the northern Gulf of California, south of O'odham country, was a highly structured ritual that only secondarily had to do with obtaining salt. The mysterious ocean, *kaachk shuudagĭ* (also called *ge kaachkĭ*) was a supernatural source of power or strength sought by young O'odham men.

The actual trip—at first on foot, later on horseback—lasted over a week. The single-file procession was led by a man who knew the ancient desert trails and several water holes and had memorized the long formal orations that must be recited at various points along the journey. His function was priestly, not shamanistic.[1] The followers were silent. The first-time participants ate and drank little, only at prescribed intervals. They each carried a **wakoa** (**vakoa**) and a packet of **huuñ hiaakĭ chu'i**, 'parched cornmeal'.

---

1. Shamanistic practices arise from personal encounters with spiritual beings or helpers. Priestly functions derive from a (usually) long process of learning from a mentor or elder. Priestly functions are community oriented, while shamanistic practices are individual focused. Among O'odham, reciting long ritual orations or narrating the Creation Story is priestly, whereas diagnosing sickness is shamanistic. Both types of practices might be involved in various O'odham ceremonies. In the past certain *mamakai* might call rain, ensure good crops, or locate the enemy on the warpath, according to each one's specialization. The primary function of a *maakai* today is diagnosing *mumkidag*.

On arrival at the shore, the leader threw cornmeal on the waves and recited an oration. The ocean also received offerings of precious *wiigĭ* (*viigĭ*), 'fluffy eagle feathers', and a prayer stick from each pilgrim. Participants must wade into the ocean and brave the waves four times. Prayer sticks are called *omina*.

The coastal setting was different from any other they had known, with strange plants and rock formations. The exhausted and thirst-crazed participants expected to receive power from close proximity to the mysterious spread-out water. Tobacco smoke might induce trance. They might also run on the beach until they fell. This contact with the supernatural might give the young man power to be a good singer, runner, gambler, hunter, or healer. It was a confirmation of vocation.

The high spring tides had left water in several shallow lagoons that had now evaporated, leaving crystalline salt deposits. After circling the lagoon four times, the pilgrims broke loose the salt, spread it to dry, then packed it for carrying back to their village. The return was a silent ritual, punctuated by formal orations. Back at the home village, the salt was ritually purified and the pilgrims underwent a seclusion for at least four days. First-time participants might have to endure a vigorous sixteen-day purification, after which they were considered adults.

Now the salt could be given away or traded to the Akimel O'odham or even sold to Mil-gan (Americans) or Jujkam (Mexicans). But as with all O'odham rituals, the ultimate goal was to bring rain to O'odham country. The ocean was considered its source.

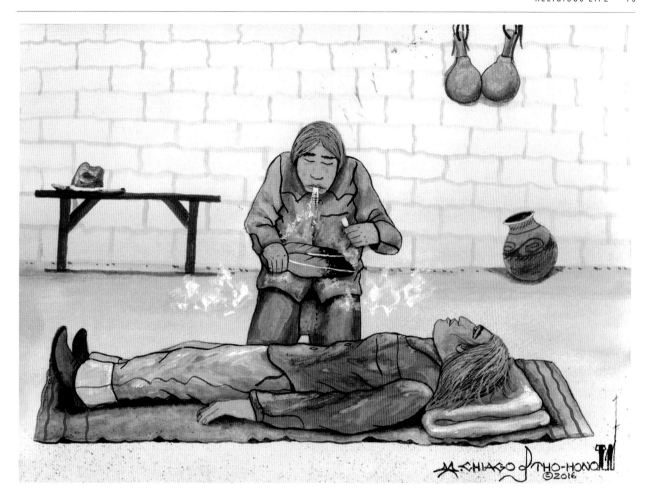

SHAMAN DIAGNOSING ILLNESS IN *DOAJIDA*

In the O'odham worldview, there are two main forms of *mumkidag*, 'illness'. One is called *oimmeḍdam mumkidag*, 'wandering sickness', which can pass from person to person and can afflict all kinds of people, even non-O'odham. These are contagious diseases. The other is *O'odham mumkidag* (*kaachim mumkidag*), 'staying sickness', which affects only O'odham or True People. *Kaachim mumkidag* has a number of varieties, is diagnosed by a *maakai*, and is cured by ritual.

   Kaachim mumkidag is acquired by some offense to a powerful or sacred being, often a bird, mammal, reptile, or insect. Only certain species are so endowed "from the beginning" with such power. *Kaachim mumkidag* can also be caused by not performing a ritual correctly or violating some of its ritual restrictions. The violation can be killing or harming an individual, or not dispatching a game animal quickly and painlessly, or not protecting its bones from desecration by dogs. Hunters in particular have to be cautious while their wives are pregnant to avoid harm that might affect the child after birth. The effects of *kaachim mumkidag* may be manifested at some later time, even in adulthood.

The role of the *maakai* is to diagnose the agent causing the illness. The violation may be long forgotten or even unknown to the person. Left untreated, the patient eventually dies from the sickness. The results of several violations might be manifested simultaneously in the patient. The *maakai* must determine which is the strongest and must be dealt with first.

When a *maakai* is called to hold a *doajida*, 'divining session', for a sick person, he attempts to identify what organism or object or lapse is causing the patient's problem. Some reported symptoms are specific to particular violations, while others are more general. Multiple violations complicate easy diagnosis. The session is usually held at night. The *maakai* uses a gourd rattle in one hand and a matched pair of divining feathers, usually from the Golden Eagle, in the other. He has a set of diagnosing songs that may last part or all of the night. These are proprietary, and he sings them in a tone difficult for listeners to interpret. The diagnosing song is called a *kuaḍk*. As shown in this painting, the *maakai* also uses tobacco smoke from rolled cigarettes and his quartz crystal to help him visualize the problem. If successful, the *maakai* "sees" what is causing the problem. For instance, he may determine that the patient has *chuk chuuvĭ mumkidag*, 'Black-tailed Jackrabbit sickness'.

For less deep-seated illnesses that are not yet strong, a shorter ceremony by the *maakai*—called a *kulañmada*—may serve to identify and remove some types of *mumkidag*.

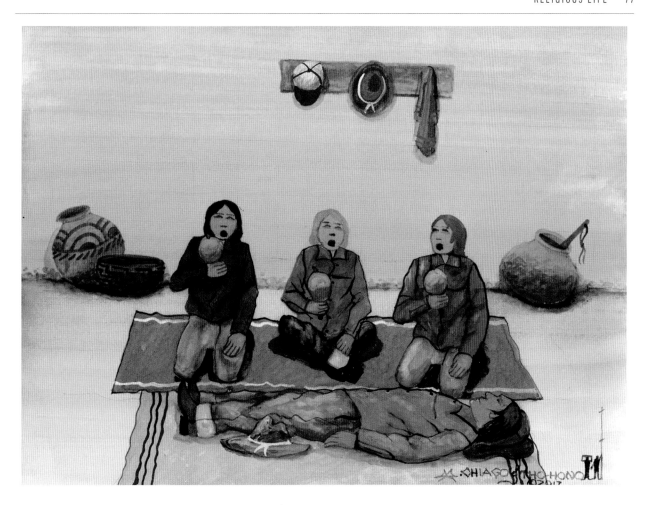

WUSOTA, 'HEALING CEREMONY'

The actual healing of **kaachim mumkidag** usually occurs in a special ceremony called a **wusota**. Ritual healers—who are not shamans—are individuals who have had an "encounter" with a certain animal or personified natural phenomenon that has "met" them and taught them healing songs. The man or woman who has met a helper is a **namkam**, 'meeter'. If, for instance, a Great Horned Owl comes to a person and gives him or her Great Horned Owl healing songs, that healer is called a **chukuḍ namkam**. The **nanamkam** can teach their songs to others. If the shaman's diagnosis is **chukuḍ mumkidag**, a **wusota** healing ceremony is arranged.

This is a public or communal ceremony, often held at night. The **namkam** and others who may know the set of curing songs then sing over the patient. The healer also may blow smoke over the patient, just as the **maakai** does during diagnosis. Fetishes, such as the paw of a badger for badger sickness, or a horned lizard carved from paloverde wood for horned lizard sickness, may be rubbed over the patient. For **chukuḍ mumkidag**, feathers of this specific owl are used. Sicknesses vary in strength according to cause and how long they have gone undiagnosed. A **wusota** for a powerful or deep-seated illness may last all night.

In this painting, three singers, called **s-wusos o'odham**, are singing over the patient. No fetish is shown, so we don't know which sickness is being treated here.

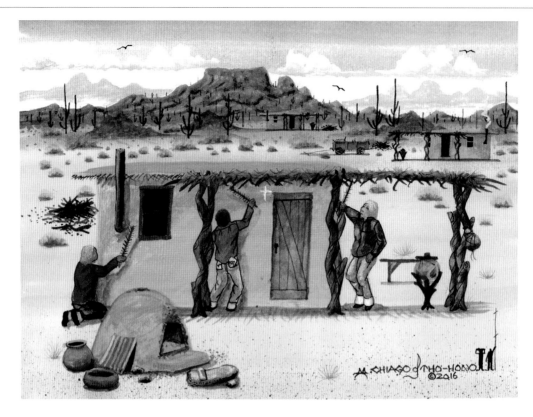

THE *A'ADA*: A VILLAGE CLEANSING

The *a'ada* ritual, literally 'the sending away', may be performed in several different ceremonies, such as the cleansing of newly harvested agricultural products so they do not give people diarrhea. In this painting, the cleansing is of an entire village.

A *sai jukam* (*sai maakai*), also called *ko'ok maakai*, 'bad shaman' or 'sorcerer', may have sent some offending object (*hivhoiñig*) into a neighboring village. (*Hivhoin* means to cast a spell.) This may be suspected because several people are suffering illnesses. A good shaman may search the village all night, supported by a group of singers. After the *hivhoiñig* has been found and destroyed, men go about the village with long *melhog* branches and beat on the outside of every house to dislodge and collect any sickness that may have escaped from the poisonous object.[1]

In the ritual oration, the Ocotillo is considered a living creature. It has been standing out on the upland bajadas, collecting wind and moisture (see the Saguaro harvest paintings in part 2). The branches are said to rumble and thunder inside. The cleansing takes all day. In Michael's painting, two old men beat the walls while a third cleans the *vatto*.

At the end, the captured sickness is brushed off the branches with a *toota hannam*, or *haḍshaḍkam*, 'Jumping Cholla'. A long oration is recited before the Ocotillo branches are buried or driven into the ground and the cholla branches burned. Now the danger has been 'sent away'.

---

1. The idea is that wind is knocked off the Ocotillo branch and attached to the house. When the rain comes, it will see its "path" and ultimately thoroughly drench and *mum kiidag keishpa*, 'cleanse the village'. (Thanks to Culver Cassa for this note.)

Rain Ceremonies

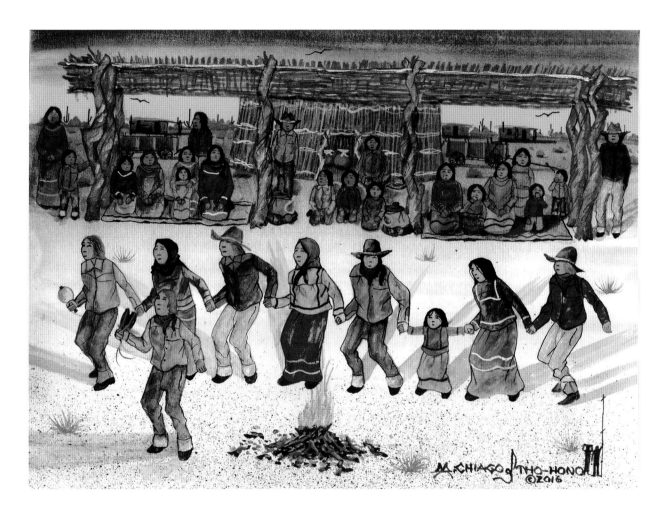

NAVAIT I'IDAG, 'WINE DRINKING CEREMONY'

After the Saguaro fruit has been harvested and boiled down to *sitol* in the camps, it is carried back to the village. Now is time for the annual wine feast, called Nawait (Navait) I'idag, or the Wine Drinking Ceremony, the most sacred and important ritual in the O'odham liturgical calendar. The summer monsoons are about to begin, and the O'odham must encourage them to be plentiful. (If storms have already begun, the ritual is to pray that they continue in order to bring a bountiful harvest.) Messengers are sent out to announce the date of the feast to neighboring villages.

People bring *sitol* to the communal round house or *wa'aki* (*va'aki*), 'rain house'. The deep reddish-black syrup is mixed half-and-half with water in large clay *navaitakuḍ* holding eight to ten gallons of liquid. These are used only for fermenting the *nawait* (*navait*). The process takes about forty-eight hours and is attended constantly by older men, including perhaps a *maakai*. They build a small fire inside the *va'aki* to keep a constant temperature, and they sing to ensure that the fermentation goes right.

As dusk comes, an official elder, *juukĭ wuadam*, shown here with a wand of Golden Eagle feathers, divines and leads the people in a circle dance around another small fire outside. This nighttime dance and divining are called *jujkida*. A hundred or more may join the circle. Their songs during the two nights are to help the fermentation; they are rain petitions and may reference toads, horned lizards, and the Red Velvet Mites—animals associated with the monsoons. The dance step is called *gohimel*.

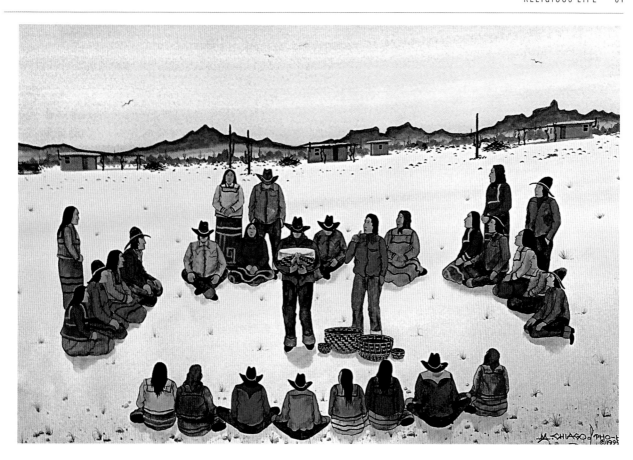

DAHIWUAK II'E: THE SIT-AND-DRINK PART OF THE WINE FEAST

After two days, if all has gone well with the fermenting (no bad shaman has interfered), the host village invites members of three other main villages to come at noon for the *dahiwuak ii'e*, or sit-and-drink part of the wine feast ceremony. There is a *daḍshpa ñiok*, 'seating speech', assigning the villages to three directions, with the host village to the west. (Of course, there were many more people than shown here in Michael's painting.)

The wine is brought out from the *wa'aki* (*va'aki*) in large, tightly woven baskets made for the ceremony. The man in charge of the fermentation or some other influential elder (shown here in blue shirt and brown pants) gives an informal speech to remind the people to be peaceful and happy while they drink, avoiding violence. Servers then move in two directions to serve the participants a cup or half a gourd full of wine.

Before all the wine has been drunk, a special narrator begins the Shuugaj Ñe'okĭ, 'Mockingbird Speech', a long, memorized oration that encapsulates all the metaphors of the wine feast and caps off the liturgy. The clouds and storms from the four directions are described, as well as the growth of crops and wild plants that is expected.

After all the wine from the *wa'aki* has been finished, the people disperse to their own homes, together with their guests from neighboring villages, to finish any *haashañ nawait* they may have brewed at home—continued prayers for the summer monsoons that made their dry farming possible.

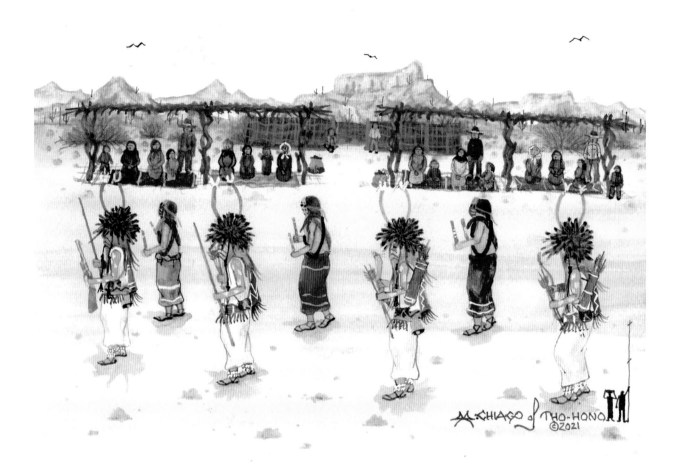

NAVIJHU DANCERS AND WIIGIDA (VIIGIDA) CEREMONY

Sometime in the historic or prehistoric past, the O'odham borrowed from the Hopi Pueblos a kachina dancer and three of his attendants. They kept the attire and much of the behavior but gave them new names. The O'odham called the primary kachina Navijhu. He wears a shoulder-to-knee kilt and a case mask of leather or canvas covers his face and neck. A leather sash provides tinklers of shell or metal. Navijhu is associated with rain and crops; he wears a broad wrist guard in which he keeps seeds. One of his attendants, a boy called the *kokshpakam*, 'snouter', wears a gourd mask with a tubular mouthpiece. Multiple Nanavijhu may perform simultaneously. They follow an unmasked *chu'i wuadam*, 'cornmeal spreader', into the dance area.

A number of other performers—the *vipiñim*, 'singers'—wear face masks of decorated half gourds. These are perforated with rows of small holes on the upper half so the dancer can see. They also wear kilts. Their bare chests, arms, and legs are spotted with white, representing kernels of corn. They swing a *wevkuḍ* (*wiwadakuḍ*), 'bull-roarer', made of a flattened and decorated piece of saguaro rib. Its sound represents the deep rumbling of the thunder that brings the rain. The name *viiñim* refers to the kachina's origin in the north.

Although often called "clowns," the Nanavijhu are not clowns in the Hopi sense, but kachinas, which have a different supernatural connotation. But kachinas can also clown, and, in this case, buffoon they do. They carry ridiculous bows and clumsily made arrows. On their begging trips on the eve of the Wiigida Ceremony, they go about the village and shoot arrows into food and other items they need for the ritual, which must then be relinquished.

The Navijhu Ceremony was once carried out in the Akimel O'odham villages where its primary function was curing, mostly arthritic or swollen legs. As with Hopi kachinas, the dancers' personal identities are secret. At Kaij Mek in Tohono O'odham country, the ceremony, called Wiigida (Viigida), was more along the lines of a harvest ceremony held every fourth year. Kaij Mek made innovations to the ceremony, shown in Michael's painting. Here, the Navijhu was crowned with a headdress of turkey tail feathers and his legs were wound with cocoon rattles, an item borrowed from Yaqui dancers to the south of the O'odham. At Quitovac oasis in northern Sonora, the annual celebration occurs in late July or August and is combined with a miniature wine feast. Its function, in addition to continuing the summer monsoons, is to make the world right and to cure leg afflictions.

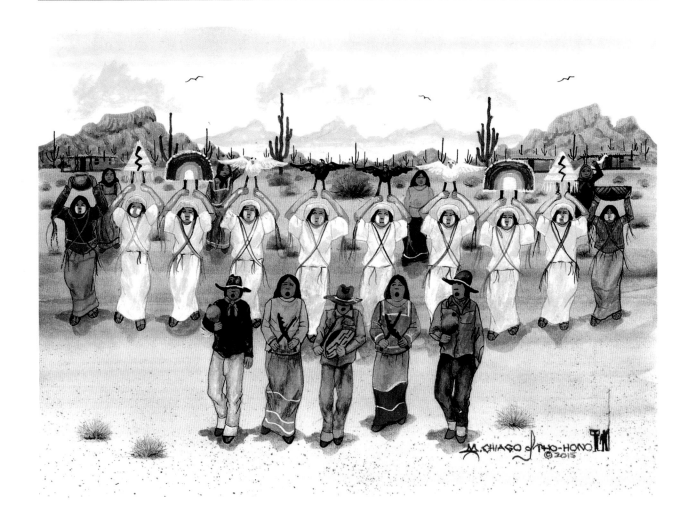

THE CHELKONA, 'SKIPPING DANCE'

There were several intervillage events involving races, gambling, feasting, and the presentation of elaborate dances. One of these dances was called the Chelkona, 'Skipping Dance', performed by the visitors for the host village.

The Chelkona, also called the Eḍa I Meḍ, was so named for its skipping step and intricate maneuvers. The performance required months of preparation. New songs had to be dreamed by a singer and taught to the choristers. Props had to be made. The choreography had to be practiced.

Around ten pairs of dancers, young boys on one side, young girls on the other, made up the performers. Sometimes they moved in double file (in a parallel line); at other times they formed a single line. Here Michael has shown just one line, without their partners.

The dancers wear a helmet of white cotton and have their faces painted in some design (it varies by performance) with white clay. Each carries an *iagta*, 'effigy', on a stick. Some represent mountains, others clouds with lightning and rain. Some carry rainbows. Others carry effigies of birds associated with the ocean (gulls) or ponds (herons and egrets). In this painting, the dancer on the left carries a *ha'a*, perhaps of saguaro syrup, while her counterpart on the right carries a *hua* (*hoa*) filled with field produce.

Leading the group are the musicians and singers. The one on the left accompanies himself with a *shawikuḍ* (*shavkuḍ*, *shaikuḍ*), 'gourd rattle'. The woman next to him carries a *hivkuḍ*, 'rasping or scraping stick'.[1] The middle man keeps time with a drum (an overturned basket) and a stick.

The songs speak directly or indirectly of rain, the ultimate blessing sought by the Desert People. The entire complex ceremony is focused on this end. Several host village women behind the performers wave their arms and handkerchiefs in joyful appreciation, as their village will be the recipient of the blessing rain.

The ceremony is still performed in an abbreviated fashion by demonstration dance groups in Tohono O'odham country.

---

1. Although Michael has shown two women holding scraping sticks, an O'odham woman would not use the *juukĭ uus* or *hivkuḍ*, let alone even touch it.

6

_

CULTURAL EXCHANGE

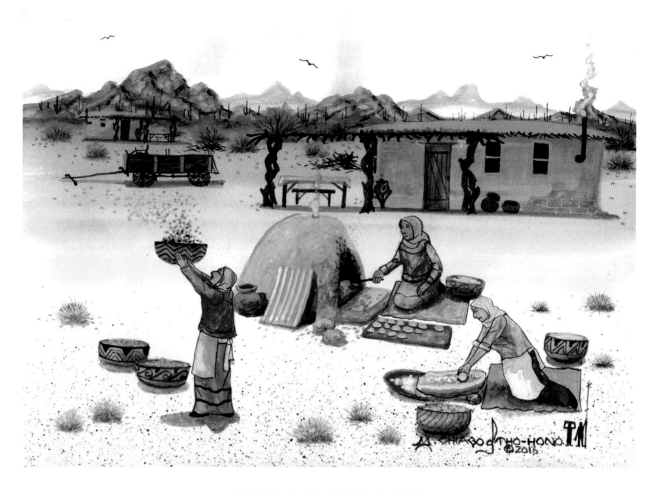

WHEAT REPLACES MAIZE

There's more to this painting than may at first meet the eye. It's a document to culture change by adaptation of new elements. The houses are rectangles of adobe brick rather than traditional *o'olas kiikĭ*. A *kalit*, 'wagon' (from Spanish *carreta*), waits to be pulled by a *kawiyu* (*kaviu*), 'horse' (from Spanish *caballo*). Tables and benches have replaced the woven mats once spread on the ground for eating. And an outdoor *ol-niio* (from Spanish *horno*, 'oven') is used for baking buns (*paan*).

But most importantly, *pilkañ*, 'wheat', has largely replaced *huuñ*, 'native corn or maize', as a daily staple. Wheat was introduced to the O'odham at least by the early 1700s at Jesuit missions. It could be dry farmed during the cooler winter months when storms brought rains from the Pacific. For the Akimel O'odham, it added a third season to their traditional double-cropping cycle. For both Akimel O'odham and Tohono O'odham, wheat became the prominent grain for making *chechemait*. (Only in the last few decades has wheat begun to replace corn on the tables of Mountain Pima and lowland Pima Bajo in Sonora.)

Wheat is nutritionally inferior to native maize. And commercially processed flours have a higher glycemic index than corn masa or even hand-ground wheat, so the dietary switch has not been all that benign to a diabetes-prone people.

For Akimel O'odham in the north, wheat became a lucrative commercial crop when Anglos and Hispanics began settling around their homelands. Various Tohono O'odham villagers journeyed north to Akimel O'odham country to help with the enormous harvest, taking some home in exchange for their own desert products. The Akimel O'odham system collapsed with overgrazing and other forms of watershed abuse in the uplands and the usurpation of surface flow due to non-O'odham agriculture and mining in the lowlands.

In this painting, one woman tosses thrashed wheat in a basket so the wind can carry away the chaff, a process called *da'ichud*. Another grinds the cleaned wheat in her *machchuḍ*, using a *wiidakuḍ* (*viidakuḍ*), 'mano'. The *hejel chu'i*, 'flour', falls into a carved wooden *chu'i waagakuḍ* (*chu'i vaagakuḍ*), also used for mixing bread dough (flour, water, and yeast). This wooden bowl, usually of mesquite, may also be called a *vajiho*. A third woman forms the dough into small loaves and puts them on the hot floor of the oven after the coals have been raked away. Then she will cover the opening with a sheet of corrugated metal.

Still, maize, particularly a quick-maturing sixty-day corn called *toota huːñ*, never lost its popularity among the O'odham, and it continues to be farmed. Roasted then coarsely ground, it is cooked into a porridge called *ga'iwesa* or *ga'ivsa hidoḍ*.

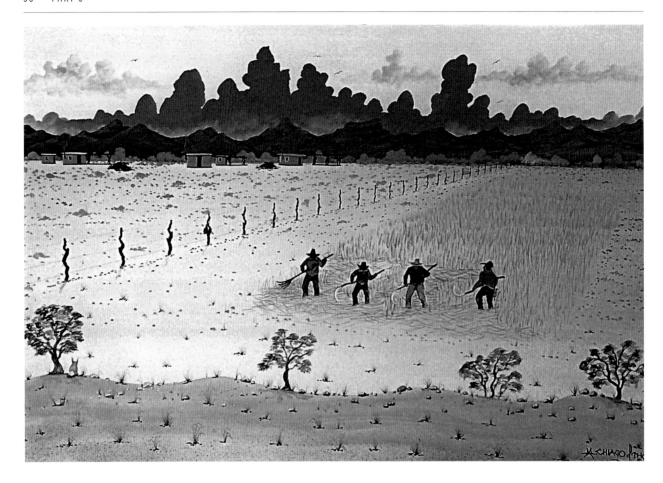

WHEAT HARVEST

With the introduction of wheat came new farming techniques. Fields now had to be protected from Old World herbivores—horses, cattle, burros, goats. Large fenced fields were plowed with a Spanish-style wooden plow. It took its name, *giikĭ*, from the small hardwood hoe that the farmer on his knees once used to break up the soil. O'odham planted wheat in hills, just as they did their native *huuñ*, rather than sowing broadcast.

In spring, the wheat was harvested by hand using an *ooso*, 'sickle'. One man in this painting uses an *olgíiva* (*ol-gíiya*; from Spanish *horquilla*) to rake the cut wheat into mounds that will be placed on a canvas and carried in a wagon to an *olhan* (*olhain*), 'threshing floor'. Here, horses are ridden in circles over the wheat, breaking it up. This threshing is called *kehivina*. Then when a wind comes, the threshed wheat, gathered into large flat tray baskets, is *da'ichud*, thrown up over a canvas, the wind blowing away the *moog*, 'chaff'. Then the cleaned wheat is stored in a large basket called a *vashom* that might hold ten to fifteen bushels of wheat, barley, teparies, or other seed crops. The *vapshom* are kept in the storage house.

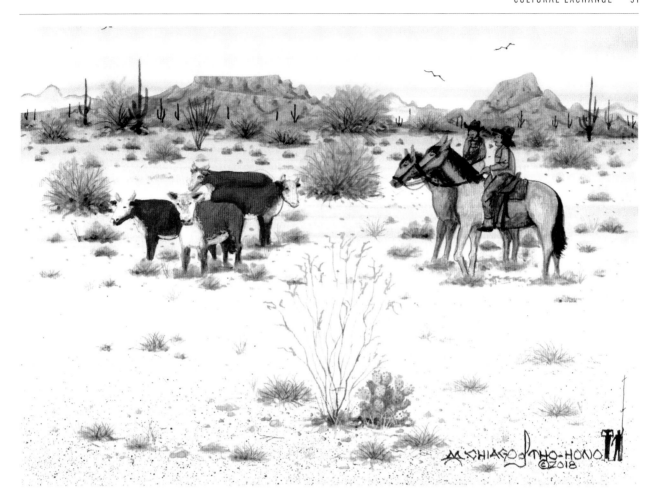

THE CATTLE INDUSTRY

The introduction of cattle and horses to the missions by Father Eusebio Kino resulted in many changes to O'odham life. The Akimel and Tohono O'odham quickly became excellent cattlemen. But there were drawbacks.

From the beginning, livestock were a magnet that attracted raids from surroundings tribes. Cattle could disrupt the supply of water for agriculture and domestic use. The cattle industry is always a risky business in desert environments; it easily led to overstocking and the degradation of the fragile desert ecosystem.

The original breed of criollo cattle the Spanish introduced was better adapted to desert conditions, but the strain was rangy. In the 1930s, U.S. government advisors urged the O'odham to replace these with commercially better beef-producing breeds. Charcos or impoundment basins were enlarged along arroyos to capture rainfall runoff for cattle.

While the O'odham became quintessential cowboys, too much attention to horses, tack, and the "good life" surrounding cattle raising was incorporated into a belief system regarding personal well-being. It could lead to *jiawul mumkidag*, a very powerful form of staying sickness. Traditional hunting largely gave way to animal husbandry. Village feast days, once dependent on rabbit drives as a meat source, now offered huge pots of hot red chile beef stew.

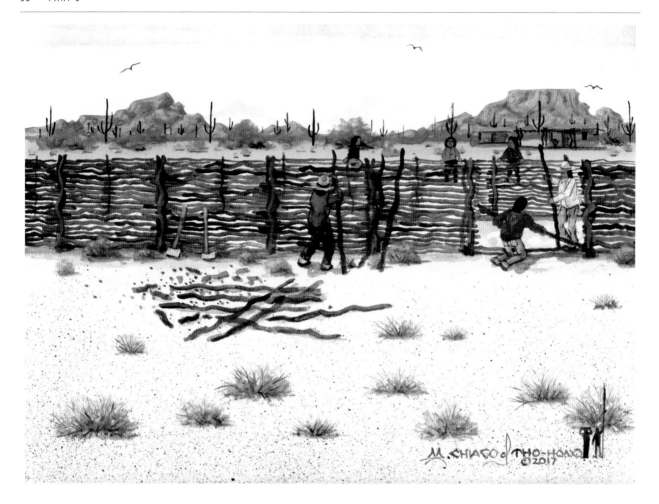

MESQUITE LOG CORRAL

Cattle and horses relished the crops of the O'odham farmers, so various forms of fencing were necessary to protect vulnerable plants. Some of these were simply spiny branches cut and stacked high (*wuis kolhi*). Others were more elaborate. For farmers along rivers and streams, the *sha'i kolhi* were brush fences, often incorporating living bushes and trees. Eventually *wainomĭ* (*vainomĭ*) *kolhi*, 'barbed-wire fencing', became the standard garden protection where livestock ranged free.

Every major village in Arizona and Sonora had an *uus kolhi*, 'corral', for the periodic roundup and branding of cattle. In the north, these were made of heavy mesquite limbs stacked in a circle. In the south, other hardwoods were used, but the design was the same. The walls were heavy and strong. But they eventually disintegrated nonetheless. Here Michael has shown the rebuilding of his own village's corral in the early spring of 2017. There had been good winter rains, so the landscape is bright green.

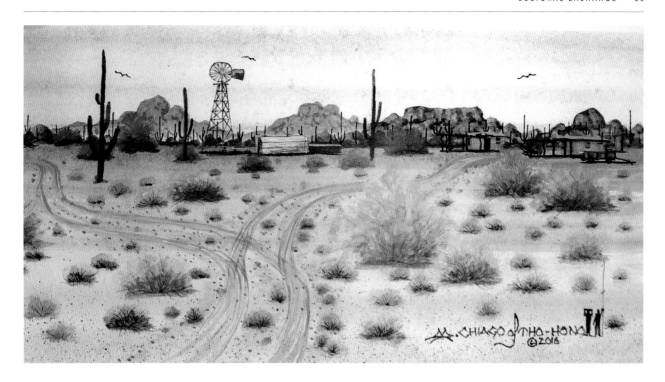

LIFE IS CHANGED BY WELLS AND WINDMILLS

O'odham living in the extreme desert of northwestern Sonora and southwestern Arizona, called the Hia ch-eḍ O'odham, or Sand People, were nomadic, moving as resources were available. The Akimel O'odham, or River People, lived along permanent desert streams such as the Gila, San Pedro, and Upper Santa Cruz Rivers with more available resources in a rich ecotone. They are the one-village people. Various groups called the Tohono O'odham, or Desert People, split their time between more mountainous villages with springs in the winter and the field villages where they could dry farm in the summer. These are the two-village people.

In the early 1900s, the U.S. government began drilling wells—thirty-two in all—in the lowland Tohono O'odham settlements, allowing permanent residence in the *o'oidag*, or field villages of these two-village people. In the 1930s the Civilian Conservation Corps (CCC) employed O'odham laborers to drill additional summer-village wells. Now many families could remain in the lowland settlements.

Many O'odham were and still are cattlemen. In this painting, Michael has shown a windmill, a source of energy for pumping, and livestock watering tanks, the white one for water storage. Now the cattle industry could be expanded and small crops raised even without summer rains. This scene shows the landscape after late winter and early spring rains from the west: the desert is green. There is food for people in the form of *iiwagĭ* (*iivagĭ*), as well as forage for cattle and horses. But as with all such technological changes in a culture's traditional ways, there was a downside: more readily available water meant more livestock, which could lead to overgrazing the fragile desert ranges.

The small outhouse, called *biitkuḍ* (*biitwuikuḍ*, *bitviku*), is another innovation.

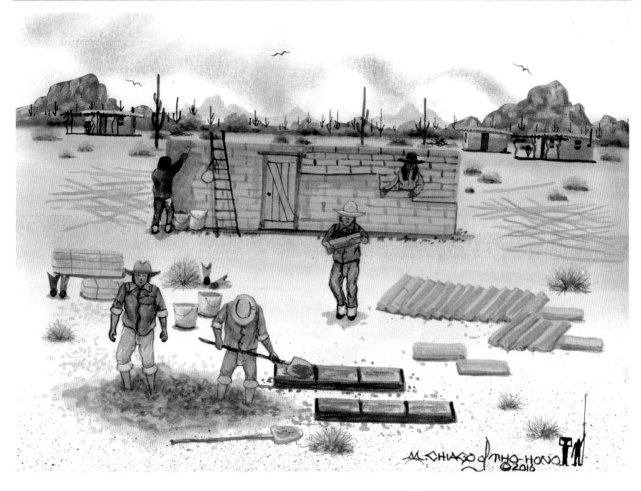

BUILDING AN ADOBE HOUSE

With Spanish contact, Tohono O'odham began to adopt adobe brick construction in place of their traditional *o'olas kiikĭ*. Adobe houses, *shaamt kiikĭ*, are more permanent, with good insulation, making them cooler in summer and warmer in winter.

Construction begins with making a supply of adobe bricks. Two men mix clay soil with *va'ug*, 'straw', and water in a pit, stomping it with their bare feet. When it is the right consistency, it is shoveled into *shaamtakuḍ*, 'wooden brick molds'. When the adobe is dry enough to hold its shape, the forms are removed, and the *shaamt*, 'bricks', finish drying flat in the hot sun. The unfired bricks are then stacked in rows until needed.

A man at the back lays bricks using more adobe mud as mortar. The doorframe supports a short lintel built into a layer of brick. Doors are made of commercial lumber. O'odham doors face east, greeting the morning sun. The man at the left is hand-plastering the new wall with *kii bidshpaḍag*, 'clay or mud wall plaster'.

Mesquite posts may serve as rafters or crossbeams. The piles of Saguaro rib or Ocotillo at the ends of the house will be used in the roof, which will finally be covered with dry earth, as in the three background houses. Often a *vatto* stands near or attached to an adobe house. A *va'igkuḍ*, 'water-cooling olla'; a *miish*, 'table', and *wuplo*, 'benches'; and even some old bedsprings and a mattress may be found in the shade of the *vatto*.

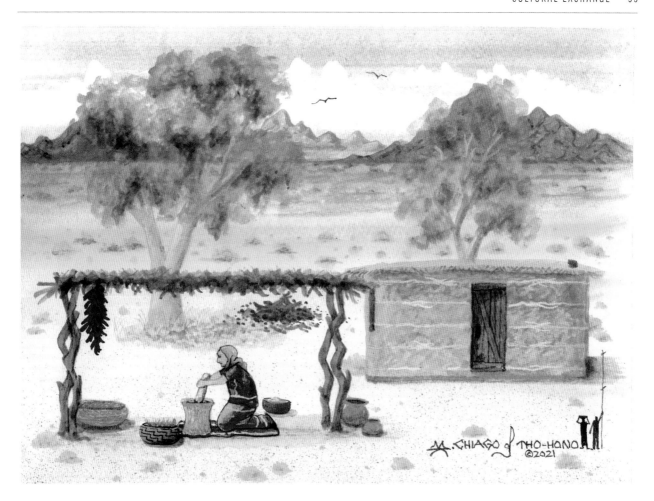

AKIMEL O'ODHAM SANDWICH HOUSE

Historic Akimel O'odham rarely made adobe bricks; instead, they constructed a light framework of horizontal Saguaro ribs or rough lumber attached to vertical posts—often old railroad ties. Then they packed the mud into the intervening space, much as in rammed-earth construction. The Akimel O'odham house was called a *shaamt kii* or, in English, a sandwich house.

A *kosin*, 'storage house', made of upright *u'us kokomagĭ* or *oagam* housed a year or two of crops, both culti-vated and wild. (While Akimel O'odham called their storage shed a *kosin*, Tohono O'odham use the word for the outdoor cooking area, closer to the Spanish source *cocina*, 'kitchen' in English.)

The grouping of houses was typically patrilocal. A man's married sons and their families usually settled close to their father's home. When a woman married, she was expected to live near her in-laws or at least in the same village.

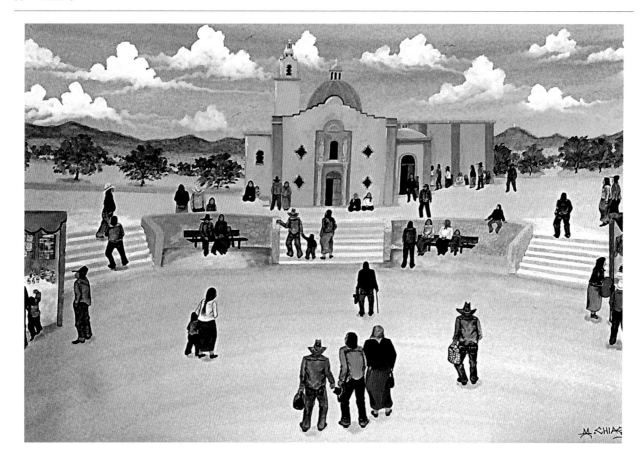

MAGDALENA PILGRIMAGE

The first week of October draws many O'odham as well as Hispanics and others on pilgrimage to Magdalena, Sonora, known to the O'odham as Malína. This was once a long trip by wagon and horseback. Some make a vow to walk the 65 miles from Nogales on the international border to Magdalena de Kino. Others today come by car. They receive a send-off from their home village and a welcoming blessing on their return. During the first few days of October, day and night, pilgrims with tired legs and blistered feet wend their way south.

The magnet of the pilgrimage is a life-sized reclining statue of the Jesuit San Francisco Xavier,[1] whose feast day is December 3. But the day celebrated is October 4, actually the feast day of Saint Francis of Assisi. The weather is better in early October, and by then the O'odham had their crops in.

The festivities, like a great Renaissance fair, last over a week and draw many thousands to the small town. Pilgrims line up for blocks around the plaza, waiting to visit the statue housed in a side chapel on the right side of the church. A carnival atmosphere pervades, with hawkers brandishing blaring loudspeakers, selling everything from blankets and household wares to trinkets and music CDs. Among the religious items popular

---

1. The Jesuits initially founded the O'odham missions of Magdalena and San Ignacio a few miles upriver, but with their expulsion from the New World in 1767, the Franciscan Order took over the mission establishments. Francisco Xavier was a Jesuit missioner to Asia, while Francis of Assisi was founder of the Franciscan Order in Italy.

with O'odham are small replicas of Francis lying in state. Herbalists, too, have set out their wares, and O'odham buy their annual supply of medicinal plants not found in their own country. Tohono O'odham congregate in their own camps in vacant lots in the local area.

While Michael has painted the scene in a rural setting with oak trees around it, the church is at the edge of an urban area and the plaza, church area, and streets at this time are packed shoulder to shoulder with visitors. Wandering bands provide music day and night. After sundown, the streets are filled with dancers, as band after band trades off.

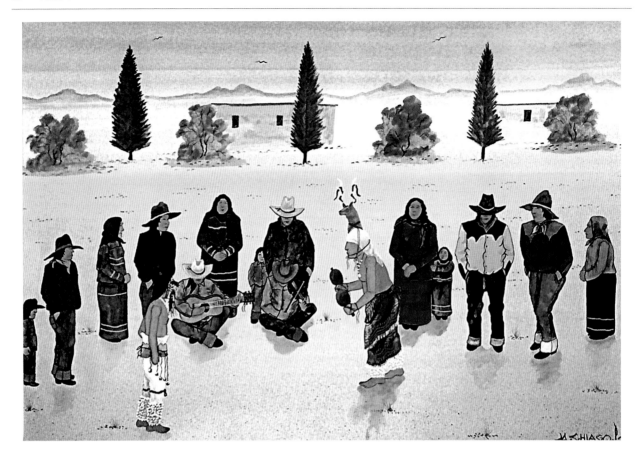

MAGDALENA AND CULTURAL EXCHANGE

The Akimel O'odham and the Tohono O'odham are the northernmost representatives of a culture area known as the Northwest Mexican Ranchería peoples. In addition to the O'odham, this culture area includes the Ópata, Eudeve, Jova, Mountain Pima, Northern and Southern Tepehuán, Yaqui, Mayo, Guarijío, Tarahumara, Cora, and Huichol. All are Uto-Aztecan speakers and share more culture traits among themselves than with surrounding tribes.

The annual festival at Magdalena in October was not only an opportunity for economic exchange but a powerful vehicle for cultural exchange as well. Tohono O'odham especially maintained strong ties to the folk Catholicism of Sonora.

In this painting, a group of O'odham have gathered at Magdalena to watch the public performance of the Yoeme (Yaqui) Pascola and Deer Dancer. Sometimes this is on the steps of the church, other times in the plaza or under the portico. The highly skilled Deer Dancer plays his two rattles asynchronistically while his musicians supply music on guitar and violin. (Missing in the painting are the water drum and rasping stick as well as the European harp.)

The Yaqui and Mayo are masters of syncretism, blending aboriginal ceremonies with Catholic ones. O'odham have borrowed the Pascola and Matachina Dancers but not the Deer Dancer (see paintings on pages 64 and 65).

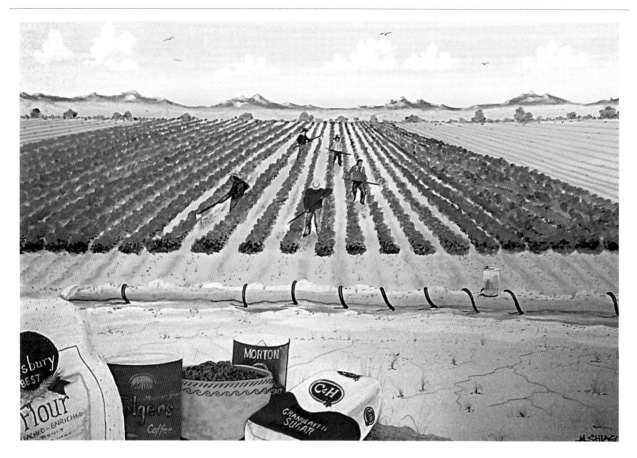

WORK IN THE COTTON FIELDS

Over the decades, many O'odham have become wage laborers in fields surrounding their reservations. Water is pumped from deep aquifers beneath the alluvial soils to grow such water-demanding crops as cotton. Leased land on several reservations is also heavily devoted to cotton raising. Fossil groundwater lies in deep aquifers beneath the desert soil. The water table is greatly pumped in excess of recharge.

The artist in his youth became intimately familiar with this wage work, which he recalls here in this painting. Sometimes workers are picked up in buses early in the morning before daybreak so that laborers can get in their hours before the midday summer temperatures get too hot. Here they are shown chopping cotton, clearing the rows of weeds. Water is siphoned onto the fields from the irrigation ditches in black pipes called *hihij*, 'intestines'.

In the foreground, Michael has shown some of the major items wage earnings are used for, such as flour for *chechemait* and commercially grown *muuñ* (different from their own teparies, a more desert-adapted species of bean). Some reservations also maintain tribal farms that are operated as commercial enterprises.

This monoculture is quite different from the small-scale intercropping of traditional O'odham agriculture that has all but vanished from the reservations.

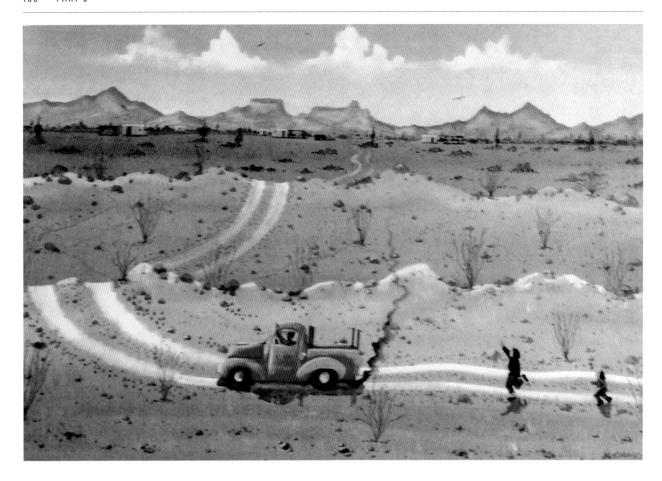

SCHOOLS

Two boys, playing hooky from school, hitchhike a ride back home to their ranchería village.

Education has been a double-edged sword among Native peoples. On the one hand, it helped youngsters compete with non-Indians in off-reservation jobs. English proficiency was a necessity. On the other hand, schools took children away at a critical age when they would have been learning the cultural ways and languages of their tribes. Acculturation was a deliberate goal of off-reservation government boarding schools starting in the late 1800s. Many of these were in other states far from home. After wells were drilled, government day schools were opened in some of the larger Tohono O'odham villages. Presbyterian schools eventually became government day schools.

Starting in 1912, Franciscan Father Bonaventure Oblasser began building not only chapels but also day schools throughout the huge Tohono O'odham homelands. He was soon joined by Father Tiburtius Wand in expanding the school system. In 1896 first a day school, then a boarding school, were opened by Franciscans in the Akimel O'odham village of Komaḍk on the Gila River. In 1943 St. John's Indian School was expanded to include a high school. The school served various tribes throughout the Southwest, but more than half were O'odham. Many tribal leaders graduated from St. John's. Michael graduated there in 1964.

If the pickup looks familiar, it's because it sat in Michael Chiago Sr.'s backyard, though he has since sold it.

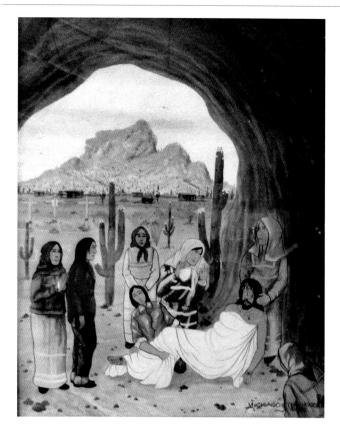

BURIAL OF JESUS AT THE TOMB

Michael Chiago Sr. was asked to paint a set of Stations of the Cross for a church in Arizona. The stations are fourteen depictions of the Via Dolorosa in Jerusalem. Like the Renaissance artists who showed biblical characters in contemporary clothing and settings, Michael painted each station situated in the Sonoran Desert peopled with O'odham.

In the fourteenth station, "Jesus is laid in the tomb," we see a cave setting with Native Americans preparing the body for burial. In earlier days, Tohono O'odham often used small caves for burials, stacking a wall of stones at the entrance. The body was protected from predators with rocks and pieces of cholla cactus. Michael's fourteenth station shows a cave burial.

Akimel O'odham traditionally buried the body in a flexed position in a chamber excavated to one side of a vertical shaft. Offerings were left with the deceased. The shaft was then filled with soil and the opening covered with *u'us kokomagĭ*, then logs of *auppa* or *kui*. Today burials are extended, but care is taken that the body faces east, the land of the afterlife as well as the source of the life-giving summer monsoons.

O'odham communities have evolved various practices to celebrate Día de los Muertos or Day of the Dead (November 2). The day before, relatives gather to clean the graves and light votive candles. Food and drink may be left out for the *kok'oi* (souls of the dead). Relatives may gather for a feast the next day.

GLOSSARY OF O'ODHAM WORDS

A'ADA   a village cleansing ritual; literally "the sending away"

AKĬ, pl. A'AKĬ   arroyos or washes

AKĬ CHIÑ   flash-flood dry farming; mouth of an arroyo where water spreads out

ALI WULKUḌ   cradle board

ATCHUDA   bottom of the basket drum, made of black devil's claw

ATOL, var. KU'UL   gravy or porridge

AUPPA   cottonwood

BAHIDAJ   fresh Saguaro fruit

BAWĬ (BAVĬ)   teparies

BID   clay

BIITKUḌ (BIITVIKUḌ)   small outhouse

BISHPADAK   horizontal hoops or stays of Ocotillo that circled the walls on the outside of the *olas kii*

CHEA (CHIA)   hail

CHEEG, var. KOMKĬCHUḌ   a hard loaf made of *vihog chu'i*

CHEEPIDAKUḌ   stone pestle

CHEEPO, pl. CHECHPO   plunge pools (*tinajas* in Spanish)

CHEHEGAM   Ladder-backed Woodpecker

CHELKONA, var. EḌA I MEḌ   Skipping Dance

CHEMAIT, pl. CHECHEMAIT   tortilla

CHEPA   a wooden mortar made of a mesquite or cottonwood log

CHETTONḌAG, pl. CHEECHTTONḌAG   vertical support post (*horcones* in Spanish)

CHE'UL   willow

CHEVAGĬ   clouds

CHOODI   a simple two-step Western dance

CHUAMA   to pit roast something in a ground oven, *chuamaikuḍ*

CHUCHK ONK   Seepweed

CHUCHUIS   Organ Pipe Cactus

CHU'I   flour

CHU'I WAAGAKUḌ (CHU'I VAAGAKUḌ), var. VAJIHO   carved wooden bowl, usually of mesquite, used for mixing bread dough

CHU'I WUADAM   ceremonial cornmeal spreader

CHUK CHUUVĬ MUMKIDAG   Black-tailed Jackrabbit sickness

CHUKUḌ MUMKIDAG   Great Horned Owl sickness

CHUKUḌ NAMKAM   Great Horned Owl meeter

CHUUKUG HIDOḌ, var. KO'OKOL HIDOḌ   red chile stew with hunks of beef

CHUUWĬ (CHUUVĬ)   jackrabbits

DAḌSHPA ÑIO'OKĬ (ÑI'OKĬ)   seating speech of the Wine Drinking Ceremony

DAHIWUAK II'E   the sit-and-drink part of the Wine Drinking Ceremony

DA'ICHUD   process in which threshed wheat is tossed in the air so the wind can carry away the chaff

DOAJIDA   divining session for a sick person

GA'IWESA (GA'IVSA HIDOḌ)   porridge

GAKIDAJ   dried Saguaro fruit pulp, either up on the cactus or fallen around the base

GEPĬ   watermelon

GEW (GEV)   snow, ice

GIAD   domesticated forms of amaranths

GIGIDAKUḌ   a special basket for sifting mesquite pod mash to make *vihog chu'i*

GIIKĬ   short digging hoe, plow

GIWULIK   constricted, belted, or cinched

GOHIMEL   dance step of the *jujkida*

HA'A, pl. HAHA'A   olla, a kind of clay vessel

HA'A-DAIKUḌ   a three-branched mesquite post for holding a *va'igkuḍ*

HAAKĬ CHU'I   pinole or parched wheat flour

HAAL   a species of squash that is at home in the hot, dry heat

HAASHAÑ   Saguaro

HAASHAÑ BAHIDAG MASHAD   Saguaro fruit moon or month

HAASHAÑ NAVAIT   Saguaro wine

HAASHAÑ SHUUD, var. HIKVIG KII   nest hole in the Saguaro made by the Gila Woodpecker or Gilded Flicker

HAASHAÑ SITOL   Saguaro syrup

HANNAM   cholla buds

HANNAM CHUAMAIKUḌ   pit or ground oven for cooking cholla buds

HA'U   gourd dipper

HAUPAL   Red-tailed Hawk

HAUPAL KOSH   Red-tailed Hawk's nest; a metaphor for kindling

HEDT   ochre or iron oxide

HEJEL CHU'I   wheat flour

HEWEL (HEVEL)   wind

HIAHA'IÑ, var. HIHA'IÑ, HIANHIÑ   sacred places or shrines; graves

HIHIJ   black pipes for irrigation, literally 'intestines'

HIKSHPI JUUKĬ   rains from gentler winter storms, but also light rains in other seasons as well

GLOSSARY OF O'ODHAM WORDS 105

HIKWIG (HIKVIG)   Gila Woodpecker

HIVHOI   to cast a spell

HIVHOIÑIG   offending object

HIVKUḌ, var. JUUKĬ UUS   rasping or scraping stick

HOA, pl. HOHOA, var. HUA, pl. HUHUA   large coiled tray baskets

HO'I   thorns

HO'IDKAM   Desert Ironwood

HOMTA, pl. HOHOMTA   large Arrowweed granary

HUA KEIHINA (HUA CHUUDKĬ), var. HOAKAJ (HUAKAJ) KEIHINA, HOAKAJ (HUAKAJ) CHUUDKĬ   basket dance

HUAWĬ (HUAI)   Mule Deer

HUHULGA KII   menstrual hut

HUUÑ   maize or corn

HUUÑ CHU'I   parched cornmeal

HUUÑ VA'UG   cornstalks

IÁ   the sweet, juicy red pulp of the Saguaro fruit

IAGTA   effigy; votive offering

IHUG   devil's claw (*Proboscidea*, Martyniaceae)

IIBDAJ   green fruit attached to the unopened flower buds of the cholla cactus

IIBHAI   prickly-pear fruit

IIBHAI SITOL   prickly-pear syrup

IIWAGĬ (IIVAGĬ)   wild greens, pot herbs

JEGOS   violent dust storm

JIAWUL MUMKIDAG   a very powerful form of staying sickness

JUJKIDA   nighttime dance and divining in the Navait I'idag

JUÑ   a cake made from pressed *gakidag* that's fallen from the Saguaro cactus

JUUKĬ   rain

JUUKĬ WUADAM   official elder who leads people in a circle dance for the Navait I'idag

KAACHK SHUUDAGĬ, var. GE KAACHKĬ   ocean

KAAWĬ (KAAV)   badger

KAIJ   small black seeds interspersed in the pulp of the Saguaro fruit

KALIT   wagon (from Spanish *carreta*)

KAWIYU (KAVIU)   horse (from Spanish *caballo*)

KEIHINA, var., CHUUDKĬ, SIKOL HIMDA   circling dance

KEHIVINA   wheat threshing

KII, pl. KIIKĬ   house

KII BIDSHPAḌAG   clay or mud wall plaster

KIKKIO   vertical wall supports of the *olas kii*

KIOHOḌ   processional arch decorated with ribbons and paper flowers; rainbow

KOḌS   a cross, including a monumental cross

KOMAL   griddle used for making tortillas

KOMKĬCHUD   Desert Tortoise

KO'OKMAḌKĬ   the Blue or Blue-green Palo Verde species

KOKSHPAKAM   snouter in Navijhu ceremony

KOKSWUL (KOKSVUL)   cocoon

KOSIN   storage house for the Akimel O'odham; outdoor cooking area (from Spanish *cocina*) for the Tohono O'odham

KOSON, pl. KOKSON   pack rats, wood rats

KOVĬ   domesticated forms of chenopods

KUAḌAGĬ   a species of ant with long, thin legs

KUAḌK   diagnosing song

KU'AGĬ   firewood

KUAVUL   wolfberry or squawberry

KUI   mesquite bush or tree, including Velvet Mesquite and Honey Mesquite

KU'IBAḌ, pl. KUKU'IBAḌ   a tool used for picking the Saguaro fruit (*bahidag*) from the cactus

KUI HIDOḌ   pudding made from flour of crushed mesquite pods

KUI HIOSIG MASHAD   the lunar month following *kui i'ivagĭdag mashad* in which the mesquite flowers

KUI I'IVAGĬDAG MASHAD   a lunar month in spring in which the deciduous mesquite sprouts fine leaves

KUI KU'AGĬ   mesquite firewood

KUI USHAB   black mesquite sap

KUK CHEHEDAGĬ   Foothill or Little-leaf Palo Verde

KULAÑMADA   a shorter ceremony by a *maaki* for identifying and removing some types of less deep-seated *mumkidag*

KU'UL, var. HAASHAÑ KAI HIDOḌ   a nutritious porridge made from *kaij*

KUUNAM   "fire drive"; a kind of communal surround

KUUKVUL   Western Screech Owl

KUUVID, pl. KUKUVID   Pronghorn

MAAKAI, pl. MAMAKAI   shaman

MACHCHUḌ, var. CHU'IKUḌ   metate or grindstone

MAIÑ   a woven mat for sleeping that is rolled up and leaned against the wall of the *olas kii* in the daytime

MAMHAḌAG   side arms of the Saguaro

MATSIG, var. MACHCHUḌ   crosspiece of the main pole of the *ku'ibaḍ*

MELHOG   Ocotillo

MIILOÑ   melon

MIISH   table

MOHO   Bear-grass

MOOG   chaff

MUMKIDAG   illness

MUM KIIDAG KEISHPA   to cleanse the village

MUMSIGO HA KII (WAILAKUḌ KII)   dance enclosure or bandstand

MUUÑ   common beans such as pintos

MUUÑ HIDOḌ   cooked pinto beans

NAADAKUḌ, var. ISTÚVHO, ISTÚÚKVA   adobe stove

NAMKAM, pl. NANAMKAM   meeter

NAVAIT I'IDAG   Wine Drinking Ceremony

NAVAITAKUḌ   large clay vessel for fermenting *nawait*

NAVIJHU, pl. NANAVIJHU   primary kachina

NAW (NAV)   prickly-pear cactus

NAWAIT (NAVAIT)   wine

ÑEI   song, a poem of four or more lines, repeated in a set pattern, then the whole set sung through four times

ÑE'ÑEI   sung poetry

ÑUI MUMKIDAG   buzzard sickness

ÑUI NAMKAM   buzzard meeter

ÑUWĬ (ÑUI)   Turkey Vulture or buzzard

OAGAM   Seep-willow

OAM BAVĬ   brown tepary

OIMMEḌDAM MUMKIDAG   wandering sickness

OLA   ball or puck used in playing *tokaḍa*

OLAS KII, pl. O'OLAS KIIKĬ   round house

OLGÍÍVA (OL-GÍÍYA)   rake (from Spanish *horquilla*)

OLHAN (OLHAIN)   threshing floor

OL-NIIO, var. PAANTAKUḌ   outdoor oven

ON   salt

O'OIDAG   field villages

O'OLAS KO'OKOL   tiny, fiery red chiles known as chiltepins in English

O'ODHAM MUMKIDAG, var. KAACHIM MUMKIDAG   staying sickness

O'OSIDAKUḌ   strainer

OOSO   sickle (from Spanish *hoz*)

OWIJ (OVIJ)   awl

PAAN   oven-baked wheat buns

PAKO'OLA, pl. PAPKO'OLA, var. PASCOLA (PAHKO'OLA)   a special type of dancer for many occasions, including the village saint's day feast

PILKAÑ   wheat

PILKAN CHECHEMAIT   wheat tortillas

SAANTO HIMDAG   local blend of Mexican Catholicism and traditional practices

SAI JUKAM (SAI MAAKAI), var. KO'OK MAAKAI   bad shaman or sorcerer

SHAADA   communal rabbit hunt

SHAAMT   bricks

SHAAMTAKUḌ   wooden brick molds

SHAAMT KII   an adobe brick structure that replaced the *olas kii* for the Tohono O'odham in the early twentieth century

SHA'I KOLHI   brush fences, often incorporating living bushes and trees

SHAWIKUḌ (SHAVKUḌ), var. SHAIKUḌ   gourd rattle

SHEGOI   Creosote Bush

SHELNA, pl. SHEESHELNA, var. SHEESHA   cut and shaved blanks of Arrowweed

SHONCHKĬ   war club

SHUUGAJ ÑI'OK   mockingbird's speech

SHU'UWAḌ JUUKĬ   fine, misty rain

SIIKĬ, pl. SISKĬ   White-tailed Deer

SISWULOKĬ (SISIVULOKĬ)   *remolindos* or whirlwinds

SITOL   syrup, usually made from Saguaro fruit

SIW HEWEL (SIV HEVEL)   'stern wind', a microburst

S-KUIG, var. KUI SHA'IK   bosque

S-MOIK ÑEOK (var. ÑIOK)   "soft talk" used in hunting oration

S-WUSOS O'ODHAM   singers who sing over the patient during a *wusota*

TAIMUÑIG   kindling

TAKUI   Soaptree Yucca or Palmilla

TATAÑIGI   thunder

TOA   oak tree, including both the Emory Oak and Mexican Blue Oak

TOBDAM   village activity coordinator or hunt leader

TOBĬ, PL. TOTOBĬ   cottontail

TOKAḌA (TOKA, TOKAL)   a game of double-ball shinny played by O'odham women and girls

TOKI   cotton, the plant and its product

TOOTA BAVĬ   white tepary

TOOTA HANNAM   Jumping Cholla

TOOTA HUUÑ   sixty-day corn

UḌUWHAG (UḌVAK)   cattail

USAGA   a 4-foot-long stick, curved at the bottom and slightly pointed, for playing *tokaḍa*

USO   a type of wooden frame

UUKSHA   circle of upright Arrowweed or other branches that provided an open-air kitchen outside the *olas kii*

UUS   bush, stick

U'US KOKOMAGĬ, var. KOKOMAGĬ U'US   Arrowweed

UUS KOLHI   corral

VAAGAKUḌ, var. VACHIHO   wooden mixing bowl

VAAMUL   marshy area

VACHPIK   coots, a kind of medium-sized water bird

VAIG   three

VA'IGKUḌ   an olla made of semiporous clay for cooling drinking water

VA'IGĬ   drinking water

VAKOAÑ   heron, egret

VASHOM, pl. VAPSHOM   special basket for storing *vihog chu'i*, and small seeds

VA'UG   straw

VAVANAḌAG, pl. VAUPANAḌAG   viga or crossbeam

VAVUKĬ   Raccoon

VIḌUTAKUḌ, var. ULUKUḌ   baby swing or hammock

VIHOG CHU'I   flour made of crushed mesquite pods

VIIDAKUḌ   mano

VII HO'I   glochids, minute cactus spines

VIIÑIM, pl. VIPIÑIM   singers

VIPIAMAḌ   stalking

WA'AKI (VA'AKI)   rain house

WAALDI   bucket

WAAMOG (VAAMOG)   mosquito

WAA'O (VAA'O)   tongs

WAAPAI (VAAPAI)   Saguaro ribs

WAAPK (VAAPK)   reed

WACHKĬ (VACHKĬ)   a small pond near the house for domestic water

WAILLA   social dance (from the Spanish *baile*)

WAILLAKUḌ   dance floor

WAINOMĬ (VAINOMĬ) KOLHI   barbed-wire fencing

WAKO (VAKO), var. WAKOA (VAKOA)   a light gourd canteen more durable than the heavy *ha'a*

WAKOLA (VAKOLA)   nitrogen-rich detritus in arroyos from animal droppings and leaflets from leguminous trees; flood-borne fertilizer

WAMAḌ JUUKĬ (VAMAḌ JUUKĬ)   strong winter rains whipped back and forth by the north wind; named after the racer, a very long and active snake well-known to the O'odham

WASHAI (VASHAI)   grass

WATOP (VATOP)   fish

WATTO (VATTO)   an outdoor arbor

WA'U (VA'U)   sweet drink made of crushed mesquite pods

WAW (VAV)   cliff or outcrop

WAWHIA, pl. WAIPIA (VAVHIA, pl. VAIPIA)   well

WEGĬ BID (VEGĬ BID)   red clay

WEPEGI   red lightning that passes from one cloud to another; the word is also used for electricity

WEVKUḌ (WIWADAKUḌ)   bull-roarer

WIHOG (VIHOG)   pods

WIIDAKUḌ (VIIDAKUḌ)   mano

WIIGĬ (VIIGĬ)   fluffy eagle feathers

WIIGIDA CEREMONY   a harvest ceremony held every fourth year

WIYÓODI (VIYÓODI)   acorn; a loan word from Spanish *bellota*

WIYÓODI JE'EJ   literally "acorn's mother"; another word for oak tree

WO'O (VO'O)   charco, a water catchment pond on the desert floor

WOSHO (VOSHO), pl. WOPSHO (VOPSHO)   cotton rat

WUAGIDA   girl's puberty ceremony

WUIHOMĬ   lightning that strikes the ground or another object

WUIS KOLHI   a type of fencing made of spiny branches cut and stacked high

WUPADAJ   cattail's flower stalk

WUSO   to blow

WUSOSIG   a healing for *mumkidag*

WUSOTA   healing ceremony

WUULO (VUULO), pl. WUPLO (VUPLO)   benches

SELECTED BIBLIOGRAPHY

Bahr, Donald M. "Pima and Papago Medicine and Philosophy," in *Handbook of North American Indians*. Vol. 10, *Southwest*, edited by Alfonso Ortiz, 193–200. Washington, D.C.: Smithsonian Institution, 1983.

Bahr, Donald M., Juan Gregorio, David I. Lopez, and Albert Alvarez. *Piman Shamanism and Staying Sickness (Ká:chim Múmkidag)*. Tucson: University of Arizona Press, 1974.

Castetter, Edward F., and Willis H. Bell. *Pima and Papago Indian Agriculture*. Inter-American Studies 1. Albuquerque: University of New Mexico Press, 1942. Reprint, New York: AMS Press, 1980.

Curtis, L. S. M. *By the Prophet of the Earth: Ethnobotany of the Pima*. Santa Fe, N.Mex.: San Vicente Foundation. Reissue, Tucson: University of Arizona Press, 1984.

Davis, Edward H. *The Papago Ceremony of Vikita*. Indian Notes and Monographs 3. New York: Museum of the American Indian Heye Foundation, 1920.

Densmore, Frances. *Papago Music*. Bulletin of the Bureau of American Ethnography 90. Washington, D.C.: Smithsonian Institution, 1929.

Fontana, Bernard L. "History of the Papago," *Handbook of North American Indians*. Vol. 10, *Southwest*, edited by Alfonso Ortiz, 137–148. Washington, D.C.: Smithsonian Institution, 1983.

Fontana, Bernard L. "Pima and Papago: Introduction," in *Handbook of North American Indians*. Vol. 10, *Southwest*, edited by Alfonso Ortiz, 125–136. Washington, D.C.: Smithsonian Institution, 1983.

Fontana, Bernard L., and John Paul Schaefer. *Of Earth and Little Rain: The Papago Indians*. Flagstaff: Northland Press, 1981.

Griffith, James S. *Beliefs and Holy Places: A Spiritual Geography of the Pimeria Alta*. Tucson: University of Arizona Press, 1992.

Hodgson, Wendy C. *Food Plants of the Sonoran Desert*. Tucson: University of Arizona Press, 2001.

Joseph, Alice, Rosamund B. Spicer, and Jane Chesky. *The Desert People: A Study of the Papago Indians*. Chicago: University of Chicago Press, 1949.

Kissell, Mary Lois. *Basketry of the Papago and Pima*. Anthropological Papers of the American Museum of Natural History 17 (1916): 115–264. Reprint, Glorieta, N.Mex.: Rio Grande Press, 1972.

Kozak, David L., and David I. Lopez. *Devil Sickness and Devil Songs: Tohono O'odham Poetics*. Norman: University of Oklahoma Press, 1999.

Lumholtz, Carl. *New Trails in Mexico: An Account of One Year's Exploration in North-Western Sonora, Mexico, and South-Western Arizona, 1909–1940*. New York: C. Scribner's Sons, 1912. Reprint, Tucson: University of Arizona Press, 1990.

Mathiot, Madeleine. *A Dictionary of Papago Usage*. Vol. 1, *B–K*. Language Science Monographs 8/1. Bloomington: Indiana University Publications, 1973.

Mathiot, Madeleine. *A Dictionary of Papago Usage*. Vol. 2, *Ku–ʔu*. Language Science Monographs 8/2. Bloomington: Indiana University Publications, 1973.

Moreillon, Judi. *Sing Down the Rain*, illus. Michael Chiago. Santa Fe, N.Mex.: Kiva Publishing, 1997.

Nabhan, Gary Paul. *The Desert Smells Like Rain. A Naturalist in Papago Indian Country*. New York: North Point Press, 1987. Reissued as *The Desert Smells Like Rain: A Naturalist in O'odham Country* with Michael Chiago Sr. cover art. Tucson: University of Arizona Press, 2002.

Nabhan, Gary Paul. *Gathering the Desert*. Tucson: University of Arizona Press, 1985.

Rea, Amadeo M. *At the Desert's Green Edge: An Ethnobotany of the Gila River Pima*. Tucson: University of Arizona Press, 1997.

Rea, Amadeo M. *Folk Mammalogy of the Northern Pimans*. Tucson: University of Arizona Press, 1998.

Rea, Amadeo M. *Wings in the Desert: A Folk Ornithology of the Northern Pimans*. Tucson: University Arizona Press, 2008.

Russell, Frank. *The Pima Indians*. Annual Report of the Bureau of American Ethnology 26, 1908. Reissue with introduction, citation sources, and bibliography by Bernard L. Fontana. Tucson: University of Arizona Press, 1975.

Saxton, Dean, and Lucille Saxton. *O'otham Hoho'ok A'agitha: Legends and Lore of the Papago and Pima Indians*. Tucson: University of Arizona Press, 1978.

Saxton, Dean, Lucille Saxton, and Susie Enos. *Tohono O'odham/Pima to English, English to Tohono O'odham/Pima Dictionary*. Tucson: University of Arizona Press, 1998.

Shaw, Anna Moore. *A Pima Past*. Tucson: University of Arizona Press, 1974.

Underhill, Ruth. *Social Organization of the Papago Indians*. New York: Columbia University Press, 1939.

Underhill, Ruth M. *Papago Indian Religion*. New York: Columbia University Press, 1946.

Underhill, Ruth M. *People of the Crimson Evening*, illus. Velino Herrera. Washington, D.C.: Department of the Interior, United States Indian Service, Branch of Education, 1951.

Underhill, Ruth M., Donald M. Bahr, Baptisto Lopez, Jose Pancho, and David Lopez. *Rainhouse and Ocean: Speeches for the Papago Year*. American Tribal Religions 4. Flagstaff: Museum of Northern Arizona Press, 1979.

Underhill, Ruth Murray. *Singing for Power: The Song Magic of the Papago Indians of Southern Arizona*. Berkeley: University of California Press, 1938. Reissued with Michael Chiago Sr. cover art. Tucson: University of Arizona Press, 1993.

Webb, George. *A Pima Remembers*. Tucson: University of Arizona Press, 1959.

Winters, Harry, Jr. *'O'odham Place Names: Meanings, Origins, and Histories Arizona and Sonora*. Tucson, Ariz.: Nighthorses, 2012.

Wright, Barton. *Clowns of the Hopi: Tradition Keepers and Delight Makers*. Flagstaff: Northland Publishing, 1994.

Wright, Barton. *Hopi Kachinas: The Complete Guide to Collecting Kachina Dolls*. Flagstaff: Northland Publishing, 1977.

Wright, Barton. *Classic Hopi and Zuni Kachina Figures*. Leiden, The Netherlands: E. J. Brill, 1986. Reissued with altered form, Santa Fe: Museum of New Mexico Press, 2006.

Zepeda, Ofelia. *A Papago Grammar*. Tucson: University of Arizona Press, 1983.

INDEX

ABOUT THE ARTIST AND AUTHOR

Michael Chiago Sr. is an internationally recognized Tohono O'odham artist and illustrator whose paintings focus on culture and heritage. He is the recipient of the Arizona Indian Living Treasures Award for his cultural and artistic achievements.

Amadeo M. Rea is an ethnobiologist and ornithologist who has conducted research on the Gila River Indian Reservation for many years. Rea has written four books on the O'odham, including *Wings in the Desert: A Folk Ornithology of the Northern Pimans.*

The Southwest Center Series

JEFFREY M. BANISTER, EDITOR